SPREADING TIME

EARLE BIRNEY
SPREADING TIME

Remarks on Canadian Writing and Writers

Book I: 1904 - 1949

Véhicule Press

Montréal, Canada

Acknowledgements

The Canada Council for the grant which gave me the time to make this book;

the following periodicals in which sections of it appeared: *Books in Canada, Canadian Author & Bookman, Canadian Forum, Canadian Home Journal, Canadian Poetry Magazine, Essays on Canadian Writing, Globe & Mail, Here & Now, Manitoba Arts Review, Quill & Quire, West Coast Review;*

the following correspondents for permitting quotations from their letters: Patrick Anderson, Robertson Davies, Louis Dudek, Robert Finch, Ralph Gustafson, Catherine Harmon, Sybil Hutchinson, Eric Nicol, Raymond Souster and George Woodcock;

the old Canadian Broadcasting Corporation of forty years ago which gave me air-time to voice some of these opinions;

the staff of the Thomas Fisher Rare Book Library, University of Toronto;

Simon Dardick, Nancy Marrelli and Ken Norris, for editorial aid;

Wailan Low and Kate Hamilton, for bringing order out of scribal chaos; Oxford University Press, Toronto, for permission to quote from *Sarah Binks*.

Canadian Cataloguing in Publication Data

Birney, Earle, 1904-
　Spreading time

Includes index.
Contents: Book 1. 1904-1949.
ISBN 0-919890-24-5 (v.1) bd.
ISBN 0-919890-25-3 (v.1) pa.

1. Birney, Earle, 1904-　2. Canadian literature
(English)—20th century—History and criticism.*
3. Canadian literature—20th century—History and
criticism. I. Title.

PS8071.B57　　C810'.9　　C80-090028-6
PR9189.6.B57

41,376

Dépôt légal, Bibliothèque nationale du Québec.
National Library of Canada, 3ième trimestre.

Véhicule Press, P.O. Box 125, Station "La Cité",
Montreal, Canada H2X 3M0.

Printed in Canada.

"It's spreading time, and once more all around me,
The air is rich, and fields are flecked with gold...
The golden spots that mark our high endeavor."
Paul Hiebert: *Sarah Binks*

Contents

To the memory of Will Birney, my father
1866-1926
& Martha Robertson Birney, my mother
1875-1950

Spring Plowing 1904-26

Like most infants, I absorbed "poetry" before I could read, without knowing what it was. My mother's musical voice brought me lovings and lamentings from her Scottish childhood. "Noo I lay me doun to sleep" and "Humpty-Dumpty" and other intercontinental chants for an Anglophone baby echoed down from a Shetland croft to my corner of the single bedroom on the Albertan ranch. At three I was prattling "Jesus wants me for a sunbeam"; at four reciting the Lord's Prayer and the Twenty-Third Psalm in the Morningside Sunday School. I can't recall anyone objecting to the absence of Canadian content.

Reading? Apparently I had, like Robert Louis Stevenson, "a talent for it". I also had parents who were largely self-educated and quick to help me teach myself. My father, taken from school and apprenticed to his own father's butchering trade in Guelph, ran off to the West at fifteen to become by turns a cowpuncher, prospector, and then a signpainter and decorator. When he left that for mixed-farming in the foothills bush he prudently retained the tools of his trade, including huge sets of celluloid letters in various styles. From these and an alphabet of building blocks, an Eaton's catalogue, a pocket dictionary, and what time my work-burdened parents could spare me, I acquired early both an ability to read and a permanent love affair with Words and their infinite shapes and sounds and meanings. By six, sustained by the pleasure of puzzle-solving, I had managed to creep with snail's pace and a slug's comprehension over vast stretches of the family Bible, the Presbyterian Hymnal, all the backlog of *Family Heralds* (the only paper we could afford), and was now puzzling out the text under the lovely engravings of burning martyrs and tortured missionaries in father's three-volume *History of Protestantism.*

By my seventh birthday, when we left the farm forever and moved to Banff, where father set up in his trade again, I had at least a leafing acquaintance with everything we possessed in print, including a fat *Ireland Picturesque, With Livingstone and Stanley in Darkest Africa,* a cookbook, pharmacopeia, home carpentry, livestock gazette and an almanac. And there was the beginnings of my own Xmas-Present Library: Grimm and *Crusoe* and *Pilgrim's Progress* and *Black Beauty.* These I revelled in, read and re-read, partly because they were so easy, after *Deuteronomy,* but mainly because all that adult fare had left me a reading freak while still a child.

Culturally, of course, I was now an Anglo-American stew, a small pot of gobbets from what had survived of my father's reading fare, casually collected in wandering bachelor years through book-scarce regions of the nineteenth century Canadian West. In all of it there was only one scrap that I now know to be CanLit: a slim clean book called *Among the Millet*, dated 1888, by somebody named Archibald Lampman. The words in it were set out like hymns but my father said this was because it was Poetry, and he liked it because it reminded him of when he was a boy back in Guelph, Ontario. Sometimes he would read to me from it, though the only lines I remember hearing with his voice around them are: "The water-bugs draw close beneath / The cool gloom of the bridge." I'm sure they stirred me because we had a little bridge over our swampy creek and I had developed a passion for lying in its shadow to collect water-skaters and tumblebugs to pop in my jam-jar aquarium. Lampman's "Heat" had proved to be nationally valid; his Ottawa Valley and my father's Grand River marsh were my swamp too; they were Canada, my only world.

Into this childhood goulash went also Happy Hooligan and other American comic strips, along with "Red Wing" and Harry Lauder heard from a magical Victor horn gramophone over at Old Lady Bell's farm. But the Holy Bible was the Book that dominated. For my mother ran the only Sunday School between Lacombe and Ponoka, and I was perforce the perfect attendant. I learned to recite larger and larger quantities of both Testaments, receiving at the end of my sixth year a gold-lettered "Certificate . . . for the Memorizing of Scripture". It was signed by the Moderator of the General Assembly of the Presbyterian Church in Canada, Toronto. National recognition for a young Canadian performer. Mother tacked it over the red roses blooming on our livingroom wall, next to the Charlie Russell general-store calendar of a ranger shooting an attacking grizzly from horseback.

Starting school in Banff began as a cultural nightmare. I am no sculptor; plasticine bored me. I was handed babybooks that insulted my soul. A disciplinary problem, I was happily kicked upstairs to Grade Three and there by great luck exposed to some quite recent Canadian fiction. Miss Dykeman, our young teacher, who had come all the way from Musquodobit, N.S., on the Atlantic Ocean (no one knew why), liked to read us stories of "her country" (as we thought of it). So I was introduced to L.M. Montgomery's *Anne of Green Gables* and *Anne of Avonlea*, and G.S. Porter's *Girl of the Limberlost*. "Popular sentimental fiction", the *Literary History of Canada* labels them now. And so they were, and far too concerned with girls, but I liked them anyway. I had red hair too, and lived in Canadian woods. I liked *Mooswa* even more, and the other all-too-humanized animals of Ernest Thompson Seton and Charles G.D. Roberts. What Jay Macpherson calls "their fuzzy natural religion" I must have found better than Presbyterianism, if I noticed it at all, and I was excited by hearing stories about wildernesses, even if they were Atlantic ones.* I needed those authors then as much as my grandchildren need Farley Mowat now. Farley, indeed, would have been better for us, but he wasn't there yet. And I benefited from them even more because there was then nothing literary Canadian at all in the official school curriculum.

The nearest we got to CanLit was Longfellow's *Evangeline* — though this was part of Real or UnCanadian Literature, along with the "Odyssey" and "The boy stood on the burning deck". Literature was for reciting, or potting for exams; it was written by deceased people in other countries, and there were masses of it. But we had also a school library in that little pre-War-One Banff (pop. 500) and it had a long shelf of shiny Everymans, Haggards and Scotts that did not *have* to be read — and Henties and Conan Doyles and Fenimore Coopers.

I determined to read them all, but was gradually diverted by more contemporary sub-literature circulating in the town. The schoolboy BOPs and *Chums*, the Tarkington *Penrod* series, and grubby paperback jokebooks (*On a Slow Train Through Arkansas*) were traded at recess and smuggled with homework into bedrooms. There was also a respectable adult lending-library, which my parents joined. So Robert W. Service and Nellie McClung and "Ralph Connor" came into the home. Their novels didn't grip me like *The Last Days of Pompeii*, but I enjoyed them because they told me stories about Canada I didn't have to write exams about, and because my parents identified with the characters and the scenes and transmitted some of their excitement to me.

If my father hadn't fallen in love with my mother in 1898 he would undoubtedly have gone to the Klondike. Now, instead, he was reading Service's *Trail of '98*. For all the woodenness of its characterizations, and stereotyping of action, I think that book was for him a consolation prize for losing his bachelorhood. Though he was too shy a man to speak them out, he already knew most of Service's ballads by heart, and when a local entertainer was billed to recite "The Cremation of Sam McGee" my father took me to hear him. It was my first realization that there was something, even if it wasn't Poetry, that was great fun when properly read out, for people in Banff anyway, and it was written right here in western Canada and about people my father maybe knew. A reward for my Service fanship came in 1916 when, my father now overseas, my mother took me with her for an Easter holiday with friends in Calgary. I was keeping a diary now; the only full-page entry in it chronicles my being treated to a silent-movie-version of "The

---

*Wm. A. Fraser's *Mooswa and others of the Boundaries* was published in 1900 and the other books cited were all published in the first decade of this century. See *Literary History of Canada*, 2nd ed., Gen. Ed. Carl F. Klinck, vol. I, 297 *et passim*. (University of Toronto Press, 2nd ed., 1976.)

Shooting of Dan McGrew" at the Regent picture-house: "Just before Dan was shot they turned out all the lights and the piano player stopped and somebody behind the curtain fired a real pistol, and everybody jumped. Wow!"

My mother, no lover of violence, preferred Nellie McClung. There were even, in those first Banff days, store-bought copies of *Sowing Seeds in Danny* and *The Second Chance* in our parlor, presents from my father, who could provide a few dollars beyond bills now we were free of the ranch. My mother when a mere child had run away from the Shetlands to be an overworked maidservant in Edinburgh. It was easy for her to identify with the little hired girl in *Sowing Seeds in Danny*, and with the whole family that moved, in *The Second Chance*, from the security of a town to a bleak homestead on the prairies. Mrs. McClung could scarcely lose with my mother, in any case: Nellie was a Methodist (the next best thing in my mother's eyes to a Presbyterian), a crusader for "temperance" (i.e. no liquor at all, except brandy for heart attacks), also for female suffrage and for the international peace which women's votes would bring. Still, it was McClung's sharp eye for the small realities of the prairie experience and her sympathetic understanding of farmer's families which brought most pleasure to my mother, and to many like her in their generation. The books of Sinclair Ross and Grove had yet to be written; my parents enjoyed what CanLit they had, and I, vicariously, with them, though I much preferred reading about Indians and Eskimaux, and turned (lacking Farley Mowat or Emily Carr) back to Cooper and Ballantyne, and *Red Cloud: The Solitary Sioux*, and Wilfred Grenfell's *Down North on the Labrador*.*

It was inevitable that "Ralph Connor" should also become a household name. The subtitle of the Reverend Charles Gordon's first novel, *Black Rock*, is "a tale of the Selkirks". In 1898, the year the book was published, my father completed his last prospecting trip through those Selkirks, and was settling down to marriage on the edge of them. My parents were probably among his first readers, and read everything he published till my father's death in the Twenties. Gordon, like McClung, had extra-literary appeal for my mother. He was a Presbyterian minister and a missionary among western Canadian Indians. And he went on to produce twenty-eight volumes without a single swearword, and all with good Christian morals. My father, however, was only a somnolent Christian and read Ralph Connor because Gordon had really moved around in the Rockies, roughed it, and had the gift of calling back those last frontier days when my father too rode the passes and climbed the ridges. In his last days Gordon was asked what it was that made him for twenty years "the most widely read of Canadian authors". He gave the answer my father would have given; "I

Red Cloud (1882), by Gen. Wm. F. Butler; Grenfell's book appeared in 1911.

knew the country. I had ridden the ranges . . . I had swum my bronco across the rivers . . . ." It was not Gordon's stagey plots and sentimental characterizings, but a kinship in mountain pioneering that made my father one of the five million who bought his first three books.

Regionalism sometimes excites in regions not intended. I still remember the first appearance of Connor's *Patrol of the Sundance Trail* in Banff during the winter of 1912-13. There is a Sundance Canyon only a couple of miles from Banff, and when a few copies of Connor's book was displayed in a window of David White's General Store there was an instant assumption among prominent citizens that Connor had written about our village. Even reading it didn't dispel this illusion with some, who were sure they had detected not only our canyon but our own Mounties. There was something approaching a local "run" on *Patrol*; the store managed to get more copies and filled a whole window with them, backed by a blow-up photo of our own Sundance Canyon, and a notice offering a free copy to the winner of a raffle. I was only eight when I tried the copy my father, never a lucky gambler, had bought, but dropped it when I found there was a soppy love story in it. But I never forgot the excitement of seeing my first window display just for a book, a book by a real live Canadian about real places somewhere, at least, in our Rocky Mountains. I had become a regionalist.

By the summer, however, I was nine and a nationalist. I can't remember how it happened, but there is the evidence — in a copy of the *Pictorial Review* for 1913: me in a Christie hat and owl glasses and skewgee knickers, over a caption that named little Alfred one of the *Pictorial*'s most successful boy agents. I had been trotting around the previous winter in the snows of that innocent village, knocking on all doors, and persistently on those that sheltered friends of my mother. I was peddling subs to a Toronto magazine with shiny paper and pix of the Balkan war, and articles about Canada's greatness, and me. I read every word in every issue, of course, though I remember now only the pictures, and that I made enough, with the subs and by branching out into sachet powders, to buy the quintessential bicycle. And with the bike as working capital I was taken on the next summer to sell Calgary *Heralds* in the tourist hotels. And what a bonanza year that was! I was too busy to read what I sold, except the headlines, but I see them still at the page-tops — especially the Herald's first headline-in-red, on August 4, 1914: BRITAIN DECLARES WAR ON GERMANY.*

Ten now, and corruptible, with a salesman's reputation, I was given the chance to sell a rationed supply of the *Calgary Eye-Opener*. Bob Edwards, its sole editor, today rates two lines under "The Folktales", in the three-volume *Literary History of Canada*, as a localizer and embroiderer of many tall tales.** That he was, indeed, but much

*See my *Big Bird in the Bush and Other Stories*, Ottawa, Valley Eds, 1978.
**op.cit., 180.

more. He was the original maverick journalist of the Canadian West, an early Albertan Will Rogers, satirist of the rising Calgary bourgeois, boob-baiter, preacher-provoker, and Rabelaisian gossiper. Like most of the Banff wives, my mother would have burned at once any *Eye-Opener* that came to her hand. My father read it, I think, in his lunch hours on painting jobs — copies supplied by bachelor workmates. Edwards put out a limited supply; it sold for a dime, and bootlegged for more. Since I made a nickel for every one I sold, and only a cent for a *Daily Herald*, I took on all the *Eye-Openers* I could get. My parents never found out that I sold the filthy rag, let alone read it, line by line, unravelling the sex-jokes with the help of a 14-year-old conspirator in pornographic crime. Before I had reached his age I graduated from newsboy to butcher's helper, in summers, and sank to new depths of exciting depravity, on the side, by renting out to senior schoolboys hard porno packets supplied by a local photographer.

Shortly after my fourteenth birthday, however, my accelerating education in CanLit and NonLit came to an abrupt halt. The Birneys moved again. By June 1918 we were back on a ranch, a fruit ranch this time, in the Creston Valley of British Columbia. All that summer and the next two, we three worked dawn to dusk raising berries, tree-fruits, vegetables, chickens, pigs, calves; fighting droughts, killing frosts, plant pests, Spanish flu, monopoly express charges, rapacious wholesalers; and through two winters of stumping, slashing, wood bucking, ploughing, repairing, and generally sweating to keep abreast of the mortgage. I don't remember finding energy, in all that time, to read a new book that wasn't on the school curriculum. Nor can I recall where I would have found one, since in the whole forty-mile valley there wasn't a bookstore or a magazine stand, or a library, public or lending. The one-room highschool I attended did not even possess its own library. There must have been books in some farmers' homes, but not in any I remember entering. My mother organized a Sunday School in Erickson; I played the organ; we had a small library of hymnals and prayer books. The Creston Valley was in general a reversal to the Morningside years. We subscribed again to the *Family Herald*.

I duly read and re-read the required texts for Grades X and XI. The Canadian history book went over the same ground as the Grade IX one in Banff, reaffirming the importance of Laura Secord and ignoring David Thompson. The poetry anthology stopped with Kipling. There was much the same array of Longfellows, Rileys, and Felicia Hemans. I matriculated without having heard of William Blake or Thomas Hardy or Henry James or Melville or Bernard Shaw. And I would have heard nothing at all about CanLit if my father hadn't, our second Christmas in the Valley, surprised me with *The Oxford Book of Canadian Verse*, which he had mail-ordered from the Toronto publishers. From it I learned there were Canadian poets actually still alive — Bliss Carman, Pauline Johnson — and the C.G.D. Roberts whose animal stories I knew.

By the end of 1920's summer my father had to face the fact that his health could no longer stand up to the unrelenting work of our marginal fruit ranch. It was put up for sale, and my parents prepared to return to Banff. I was now sixteen, a farm labourer without a farm or an alternate prospect; winter was on the way. There was, however, a bank in Creston, and its manager needed a junior clerk. When he saw in the local weekly that I had led the matric exams for the region, he offered me the job and I jumped at it; even $45 a month would help the family larder.

There was a tiny "staff sitting room" over the bank, with a Morris chair and, astoundingly, a shelf of books. The other employees all lived in Creston but our ranch was an hour's biking away, so I would bring my lunches and eat them beside the precious books. Most of them proved to be, logically enough, about banking (about which I was already beginning to develop a strong uninterest); the rest were sport fishermen's memoirs of New Brunswick rivers. I read them all, of course, and was into an automatic second run-through when I was transferred 200 miles away by paddle steamer and train to another fruit valley, the Okanagan, and the town of Vernon.

My salary was now $55 a month, but the cheapest boarding house was $45. I put up with the alternative — living in an unheated unfurnished room over the bank, eating one good meal a day in a restaurant, and taking sponge baths out of the coldwater basin in the staff toilet. In this bank the only books were ledgers, and there was no socializing between the Vernonite staff and the two "foreigners". The other was the teller from Revelstoke, a friendly soul who sometimes took me for rides on his motorbike. Otherwise I endured the monotony of my trivial duties, the loneliness, and the absence of books by starting to write my own CanLit — reams of letters, diary notes, and bad verse. I flushed everything into the Vernon sewer system on the day in March when I saw I had now just enough cash to get back on the train to Banff. I resigned.

The only cultural activity I indulged in which proved to have an eventful consequence was listening to classical records in the local music store. I had made friends with the youth in charge of the playback room, a fellow-loner. He was paid almost as little as me, came from Kamloops, and knew virtually no one in Vernon — except the girls outside the town limits who had set up a lively and surprisingly economical bordello. It was the night before I was to leave Vernon forever. I had bought my ticket, and still had five dollars left for meals on the train to Banff. My music-room pal walked me over to meet June and her housemates. It became a choice between them and eating on the train. I decided it was worthwhile starving tomorrow if I could lose my virginity tonight, a decision I was fortunate never to regret.

The next year and a half, based in my parents' home, a log cabin now, in Banff, went in a scramble to help the family keep eating, and still build my grubstake for college. I was by turns an apprentice paper-hanger and painter (to my father), chain- and-rod man with a Water-ton survey party, pick-and-shovel and sledge-hammer man on a road crew, mountain guide, fossil hunter, axeman and oiler in a mosquito-control project. What little energy I had left for reading went to pulps from the village news-stand, and pop science mags. The only Cana-dian writing I can recall in all that time was Leacock's *Literary Lapses*, lent by a neighbour. I was surprised he was sometimes funny, but still preferred Bob Edwards.

In September '22 I made it to the University of British Columbia (at that time a huddle of outpatient wards on the General Hospital grounds), intending to be some kind of engineer, geological, chemical maybe. First, however, there was a compulsory year in the Arts Fac-ulty, including two hours a week of Lit. The course ranged from Euripides' *Bacchae* through Poe's "Gold Bug" and George Eliot to Shaw, an unknown and exciting stew that quickly revived my appetite for literature. The only disappointment was the collection of verse laid on for study, *Poems of Today*. Even its title was a fraud; everything in it had been written before I was born, some of it fifty years ago. All the poets were English-English, except a rather soppy Irish-Englishman (the very early Yeats). No Scots and, of course, no Canadians. The English all seemed very tame and sugary compared with the *Bacchae*, or even with my 1913 *Oxford Book of Canadian Verse*, which had masses of what to my hillbilly taste was just unsalted rhyming, but the "Cana-dian content", though nearly all Down Eastern, had made me more aware of early Canadians as real people. I responded to the satiric bite of old Alex McLachlan and the peasant humour of Drummond. And there were few poems of the Georgians that moved me as much as the Isabella Crawford selection in Campbell's anthology.

One particularly silly jingle in *Poems of Today* I have always remem-bered not for itself but for its chance effect on our whole student body. This was Sir Henry Newbolt's "Drake's Drum", enshrining a legend that whenever foes threaten Old England, the ghost of Sir Francis Drake begins thumping a drum under the Channel. I can still recite its opening:

Drake he's in his hammock an' a thousand mile away
(captain, art tha sleepin' there below) . . . .

but I remember even better the parody that superseded it on our rudimentary campus that year. It happened that Sir Henry himself arrived in our midst, fresh from Australia, in the course of a "speaking tour" of the Dominions. He was sponsored, I think, by the British Empire League back in London. Most of our older males were veterans of the world war which had just ended four years earlier. Sir Henry quickly launched into a memorized piece of patriotic oratory, blending it smoothly with recitations of his own poems (an easy enough task). When he began beating out "Drake's Drum" the veterans broke into rounds of booing. Their buddies on the staff of the student weekly rushed out a special to report the event with anti-imperialist glee, and to feature a fresh and faithful parody, struck off the same day by a sophomore, entitled "Henry's Horn". It began:

> England sent an orator six thousand mile away
> (Far away and very far below)
> To trumpet to the colonies at forty bob a day
> (Far away and very far below)

and went on from there. A glorious varsity row followed. Newbolt, now in Edmonton, wired demanding apologies. The President sent abject ones, the students none. The Prexy then fired the *Ubyssey's* editor-in-chief, and the entire staff resigned, spreading campus indignation and a faculty civil war over freedom-of-press for students. I was still a backwoods loner, and all this was an immense stimulus. I began to realize that poetry, whether bad and serious, or mocking but clever, had powers to provoke battles over ideas, rouse basic emotions, stir people to action. Out of "Henry's Horn" a flourish had been sounded I would never forget, an assertion of cultural independence, however negatively meant — a piece of *Canadiana*.

The Newbolt incident also awakened in me forgotten desires, formed in my *Calgary Herald* and *Eye-Opener* newsboy time, to be "some day" a real newsman. Continuing to read the now somewhat tamed *Ubyssey*, I realized it remained a potential learning-stage for journalists. Though I was still excited by theoretical science, my lab-marks in physics were teaching me I didn't have the mechanical talents to be an engineer. I decided to stay in Arts and train to be a research geologist. Meantime I tried out for next year's reporter staff on the *Ubyssey*, and was accepted.

Futurities, as usual, could be realized only if I made enough bucks in the approaching summer. Luckily, I won a scholarship — covering textbooks and fees — and got my job back with the mosquito gang in the swamps west of Banff.

May through September I passed in happy illiteracy, a "straw" or working-boss of a four-man crew, brush-cutting and swamp-draining around the Vermilion Lakes all week, and climbing mountains for the hell of it on week-ends. The only books I cracked were my biology and paleontology texts for the courses ahead, and my *Oxford Canadian Verse*. The previous winter had been my first experience both of Vancouver and the Pacific Coast. I was now nineteen and believed I would never grow different, would always be, like my father, an "outdoors man". I turned back to Campbell's book simply because I could find in it satisfying descriptions of wilderness things approximating what I knew, not "western" of course, but North American at least. I hunted for "good lines" in Carman, Roberts, Pickthall, but found richer rewards in Crawford again, and now also in Duncan Campbell Scott. I was settling down cosily with the Maple Leaf School out of ignorance of the best poetry of my own century.

Second year EngLit at U.B.C. did nothing to dispel that ignorance, for it started with Chaucer and dwindled away somewhere around Byron. There was an extra half-year without credit, given by Dr. Sedgewick, the department Head, that took us down to Hardy, but there was no American Literature or anything from the 20th century. By the end of my second year in Arts I was barely aware of Walt Whitman and Robert Frost, and had never heard of Pound, Eliot, Dos Passos, Sherwood Anderson, Cather, Mencken, Fitzgerald, Dreiser, Cummings, Marianne Moore or even Herman Melville. Nor did I know that powerful anti-war poetry had been written by Britishers. Sassoon, Edward Thomas, Herbert Read, Owen, Graves were not in *Poems of Today*, nor were Hopkins, the Sitwells, or D.H. Lawrence.

Most of this appalling blankness in a sophomore Arts student in 1924 was of my own making. I put little effort into reading outside the English department's narrow curriculum because I was still compulsively busy with three science courses, trying to keep my grade rating up to scholarship levels, reporting for the *Ubyssey*, swimming, weekend mountaineering, as well as girl-chasing, beering, and other routine undergraduate diversions. My friends were not really "literary", the U.B.C. library was only a starved embryo, and I couldn't afford to buy books. I would probably have gone on irretrievably into geology if it hadn't been for my casual decision to sit-in on Sedgewick's extra course, and my promotion at the end of the spring term to an associate editorship on the *Ubyssey*. The latter event put stiffening into my shaky hope of making a living as a journalist, if necessary; but it was the spell that Garnett Sedgewick laid on me that led me to abandon science and sign myself into the Honours course in English Language and Literature for the next two years. I had A's, but no excitement, from science. From even Victorian literature as Sedgewick taught it I was getting wit, sophistication, artistic standards and value judgements. I felt I was being armed for a professional life in the research and teaching of literature. This little Nova Scotian with a Harvard Ph.D. shocked parish-pumpery and intellectual laziness out of me, and replaced it with Arnoldian love for the "best that has been thought in the world". The first effects on me were to put earlier Canadian literature into more realistic perspective and yet be on the alert for what was being written at present in Canada.

That wasn't easy to discover. Vancouver still had only rudimentary bookstores; the campus had simply a textbook counter; available magazines downtown were nearly all foreign; I never heard of the *Canadian Forum* or the university quarterlies till I came to Toronto. There were, however, a few fellow-students attempting their own CanLit, some of them colleagues on the *Ubyssey*. The sonnets they published in it were certainly much more polished and eloquent than my own secret attempts, and I was still naive enough to think their authors were all headed for enduring fame, in Canada at least. (None of them were).

On the strength of my being accepted for English Honours, I was invited to apply for membership in the Letters Club, an upper-years' nest guarded by a membership committee of English professors. Required to present a paper, I asked the girl-president to accept Marjorie Pickthall as a subject. Canadian writers were not normally thought worthy of the Club's attention but I honestly thought that both her novels and poems showed considerable talent which would have led to greater things if luck had given her sounder health and more years. The fact that she had moved to Vancouver after the War and had only recently died there did arouse the executive's interest, but the advising professors decided the subject was too slight, and I was required to write, and duly presented, a paper on Rupert Brooke.

The English department's low valuation of Canadian writers was deepening my own doubts about most of them. In the case of one apparently prominent poet, doubts became certainty when he visited our campus in November of that winter and gave a noon performance in our largest classroom. None of us English students had heard of him until the Vancouver papers began giving him considerable advance publicity. His name was Wilson Macdonald and he was from Ontario. He was sponsored by the Canadian Authors' Association, the Native Sons of Canada, the *Industrial Review*, the Vancouver Poetry Society, the Alumni's University Literary Society, and the Lieutenant-Governor of B.C. It was said that he had given scores of "recitals" across Canada already, and was engaged to give more throughout B.C.

Macdonald was even worse than Sir Henry. Not only were his poems sentimental, clumsily rhymed, bathetic and often plain childish, he interlarded them with tedious self-praise. Even Dr. Fewster, whose own mid-Victorian effusions had raised him to the presidency of the Vancouver Poetry Society (a well-heeled West End gathering of culture-vultures), was so exasperated by Macdonald's "insistence both in public and private on the idea that his poetry cannot be equalled" that he would no longer give him house-room and moved him out to a local hotel. Fewster then wrote Macdonald's Toronto editor, Lorne

Pierce, begging him to discourage his author from giving further recitals in British Columbia, in view of "the antagonism he has aroused in Vancouver."*

We U.B.C. students knew nothing, at the time, of these back-stage reverberations but hadn't needed to hear them to make up our minds about Wilson. I think what annoyed us most was that, after his boring and egotistical performance, he commanded what remained of his audience (maybe about thirty) to remain seated until he had walked down to our only exit door to "greet every one of you"; at the exit he had already arranged, with the janitor's help, a money box and a pile of his books on a table placed to narrow the exit space to one person at a time. To escape, each of us had to shake his right hand while he kept one of his books at the ready with his left.

The summer of 1924 brought me into personal dealings with CanLit considered as a commodity. Since there was no mosquito control work at Banff that summer (our project had been too successful) I was out of a job. I grabbed the first one that came along in Vancouver, with a new sales-crew selling subscriptions door-to-door for *Maclean's*. We were hired with a guarantee of pay at the end of two weeks, whether we got subs or not. The first day a tough-talking professional sales-organizer briefed us on the editorial policies and plans of the magazine, the range of its contents, and the various bonus-deals we could offer. The central idea we had to get over was that *Maclean's* was both Canada's National Magazine and a journal of "international" articles and stories. We were given back copies of the two April issues to "read completely" over-night.

I was somewhat cheered by the April first issue. Its cover held a two-colour photo of a lake in "my" Rockies, and it was by a Banff photographer, Byron Harmon. Also there was an article by a Canadian veteran who had "re-visited Vimy Ridge", which my father read with a survivor's mournful interest. However, this seemed to be the total Canadian content of the issue. The major space was taken up with pop American fiction: an E. Phillips Oppenheim serial, a Norman Reilly Raine short story set in some city with "the faint, sickly smell of the Orient", and another by an equally slick writer of mindless romances, Beatrice Redpath — "Always Twenty: the vivid story of a girl who didn't grow up". As for the "international articles", apart from the Vimy travelogue, they were merely digests of articles which had already appeared in British or American journals some months before. The April 15 issue had an *ersatz* Satevepost cover of a tiny toddler holding a giant Easter egg. Both issues lacked any Canadian fiction or anybody's verse, but they did carry special sub offers: Send in a $3 sub and get *Maclean's* for a year plus an A.S.M. Hutchinson novel or

*v. Stan Dragland: *Wilson Macdonald's Western Tour 1923-24*, Coach House Press, 1975.

Ralph Connor's "latest masterpiece", *The Gaspards of Pinecroft*. Send in 3 subs and get TWO Hutchinsons.

The next three days I spent plodding from door to door in a New Westminster suburb, accompanied by a perpetually enthusiastic and cunning "senior salesman", a fast-talking and charming Dubliner. We took turns giving the pitch. By the end of the third day he sold ten subs, I none. I continued alone for another week gloomily determined to last out till cheque-day and then quit. But suddenly I began selling. Perhaps it was because the May Day issue seemed to have Canadian content, and I could fob up some belief in our National Mag, or because this issue appealed to local pride with an article on Robert Dollar, a rich American who had saddled his name on a settlement only a few miles from New Westminster (Dollarton, where Malcolm Lowry was later to be a squatter), or perhaps it was just the Haskell Coffin cover girl. Whatever sinister magic was at work, I was soon signing up enough innocent housewives every day to be continued on salary with a higher commission and transferred to a "choicer" district in Vancouver itself.

My gloom lightened, but still hovered over every street I tramped. What was I doing to myself? I had given up science and resolved to become a professor dedicated to the propagation of the best in literature. Now I was out peddling junk writing. Surely I could get the cash to pay my fees some better way than by persuading trusting housewives that literary kitsch was not kitsch if it was Made in Canada. My self-respect, never very strong, was turning to self-contempt. And my conscience nagged me because I was a working-class boy: the slicker I made my pitch for *Maclean's* as both the most entertaining and the most reliable instrument for cultural self-improvement, the more I sold subs to people who couldn't really afford them. It was only the magazine's editorial promise that an eight-pack of new Rudyard Kipling stories would commence in the May 15 issue that let me wrestle my guilt down for another week of hard-sell canvassing.

The first of the Kipling series, "The Janeites", proved to be a genuine "first" for the magazine. But the story was tedious with over-craftiness, improbable plotting, and a now unfashionable romanticism about war. It was better fare, of course, than the vacuous new Oppenheim serial about "a public stenographer in New York who gets mixed up with international intrigue" in Monte Carlo, etc. As a salesman I had to be grateful for one of the two Canadian stories, but only because its author lived in Vancouver; it was a calculated piece of early soap-opera by Isabel Eccleston MacKay: "Maria feared baldness more than death", it began. A relief, after all this, was to read Robert J.C. Stead's "The Smoking Flax"; though two-dimensional and sentimental ("a story with many heart-tugs", ran the caption), there was a real Manitoba farm in it.

I was haranguing half-open doors with the first June issue — Kipling, Joseph Lister Rutledge — "and next issue we will have a new Ben Ames Williams serial located in districts of New England well-known to thousands of Canadian motorists", and another Kipling, and maybe Somerset Maugham, and certainly the internationally famous Canadian, Arthur Stringer. And a free copy of Rafael Sabatini's *Sea Hawk* if you buy an extra subscription for a friend. . . . I was about to pass an empty house when I noticed a painter working on it from a ladder — a captive audience! I walked in and chummed him up with painters' talk.

During the dialogue that followed I learned he was a mortgage company's clerk, just replaced by a machine, but kindly kept on staff rolls, at reduced salary, painting foreclosed houses. This was before the days of rollers and sprays; he didn't know how to handle a brush and was doing a terrible job on everything under ten feet; above that he couldn't go because he was deadly scared of heights; they'd sent him a partner who quit after the first day. He didn't need a *Maclean's*; he needed a young rockclimber and dauber like me. We knocked off and went downtown to his mortgage boss. I talked that harassed fellow into letting us paint on contract, and mailed my last sub-stubs to the *Maclean's* office. The rains held off and the deal was so profitable I came back to U.B.C. at September's end driving my first car, a 1918 model-T, with enough over for fees, room — board at my parents and new clothes — and with a deep-seated distrust of maple-leaf literature.

I was too busy in my third year, anyway, for more CanLit. Though there was now a first rudimentary course in AmLit, there was no room even for that in the packed curriculum of Honours English. Critical faculties and eye-energy for the next two years had to spread to cover Old, Middle, Elizabethan, Restoration, Eighteenth Century, Romantic and Victorian EngLit (no final exams on the dubious stuff after Good Queen Vic). Anytime left over was earmarked for the *Ubyssey*, of which I was now an associate editor, fobbing up news, editorials, doggerel for the Muck-a-Muck page, and proofreading.

Only once that autumn did I try to write a "real poem", something begun in the head on a starry night on Grouse Plateau, looking down at the lights of Vancouver. I typed it out and addressed it to the Vancouver *Province*. I was too self-doubtful even to read it to my girlfriend, and I carried the envelope in my pocket for a week before screwing up the courage to stuff the crumpled thing in a mailbox. It came back, of course, with a stern letter from the ancient Literary Editor. "Since you think so little of your work that you send me this soiled, wrinkled and badly typed specimen, you will not be surprised that I think the same. . . ." Though I was crushed I was too stubborn to throw it away; fifteen years later, under wartime compulsions, I dug the "specimen" out and re-wrote it; it was published (in Toronto) as "Vancouver Lights".

My own attempts at CanLit are another story, and I mention this instance here only because it illustrates one reason why a young would-be writer in the Twenties, especially one still loaded, as I was, with the inferiority feelings of a Banff hillbilly, might be steered by Higher Education away from either a creative or a positive-critical approach to the literature of his own country. True, I was in a "cow college", but it had already attracted professors of quality, even especially in the English Department. Of its six full-time teachers, three including the Head, were Harvard Ph.D.'s; the others were a *Docteur ès Lettres* from Brussels, an Oxford M.A. with a London doctorate in sight, and a Harvard M.A. Good scholars and competent expositors, and most with eastern Canadian upbringings, their combined influence on me was enormous; Sedgewick himself remains in my memory the most brilliant and inspiring teacher I ever encountered, and one of the finest of human beings. These men, however, had not chosen me to be a creative writer but to be in my turn an erudite interpreter of the language and literature of Great Britain. Whatever had been written by Americans, Canadians, Australians, etc., in their sort of English was, though sometimes interesting, not the Best, not primary. It was the British Best they wanted us to carry through life, as they had, absorbing it so thoroughly as undergraduates that we would win scholarships to a good graduate school — we hadn't even a bad one yet at UBC — and add the higher degree that would ensure us (in those far-off pre-Depression days) a professional career even as good as theirs. (None of us, in fact, ever got to Harvard.)

Looking back now, I'm sure any one of my UBC professors would have given me kindly attention if I had brought a poem of mine for private criticism, but at the time I believed I would get only ridicule, even reprimand, for wasting energy better devoted to Chaucer-Spenser-Shakespeare-Milton-Swift-Austen-Wordsworth-Browning. My professors had created a preferential tariff in foreign literary products, and the touchstones of Matthew Arnold which Kittredge of Harvard had passed on to them, as they to us, were the trademarks guaranteeing the quality of these commodities. Touchstones? The few shiny pebbles I'd found so far in CanLit did not lead to nuggets. And it was plain that anyone aspiring to be one of Canada's literary alchemists would need to spend his probably short life elsewhere than in academic halls.

I should acknowledge, however, that Sedgewick himself did, under pressure from some of us, agree to offer a small half-term no-credit seminar in The Short Story, and even to read stories of our own in place of academic essays. All our efforts, however, came back with dis-Honourable grades and agonized Sedgewickian scribbles in the

15

margins. Soon the seminar was converted to a lovely escape-hour when he would read us a favourite tale from Conrad or Hardy, Kipling or de Maupassant, illuminating the story's craft with asides, in his soft wise voice. On the last day he begged us never to submit any of our own stories to any magazine. Especially not to a pulp magazine, because ours were bad enough to be taken, and their appearance in print would ruin forever our credibility as intending teachers of English literature. Write if you must, he said, but print nothing until you have professorships with tenure. He was only half-joking.

I told myself, however, that even if I was to forget "creating" I was still going to keep a lookout for the not impossible someone else who might be already inventing something really terrific, even in CanLit. My father, seeming to divine something of what I was feeling, presented me that Christmas with the most recent edition of Watson & Pierce's *Our Canadian Literature.** Most of it was as pallid as I had feared, but the selections from Isabella Crawford and Duncan Campbell Scott re-confirmed my belief those two were worth any Canadian reader's attention; and I owe it to my father for becoming aware there was a novelist in the country who could write with realism about prairie farming (his name at that time was Grove), and another man in the farthest East with the unpoetic name of Pratt, who had nevertheless written a moving and original poem called "Newfoundland".

That winter of 1924-25 I came also to know a live Canadian writer and be friended by him. He is already forgotten with his generation, for his work travelled to few beyond the West Coast, and his achievement was limited; yet I see now that he represented a hundred others writing in Canada, in the first part of this century, in his belief in the possibility of a significant Canadian literature. His life-long attempts to create it helped prepare the way for the far better writers in our country today.

He was a tiny gnome of a man with long gray locks and a round arched nose, whom I got chatting with one day in the university stacks, where he was an underpaid assistant librarian. He brought out for me two miniature chapbooks he had written (and published at his own cost) called *Little Lanterns.* They were wispy whimsical verses, somewhat Chinese in feeling, charming and witty as their author. His name was Lionel Haweis. He told me he was now writing ballads based on West Coast Indian legends but his main interest would always lie in Hindu mythology. He had been a planter of tea and cocoa in Ceylon.

Shortly after, he invited me and several other undergraduates who were writing, to a Sunday tea in his home at which we organized a sort of literary Exchange, for the mutual aid and criticism of our own crea-

*Published by Ryerson; the first edition had appeared in 1922.

16

tions, a non-Letters Club. At his suggestion we called ourselves The Ganesha, followers of the Indic god Ganesh, "He of the Elephant Head, Remover of Obstacles." While it lasted it was a lovely half-secret society, a dozen of us all determined quietly to write our own thing, but needing to share what problems we had in the doing of it.

We were united too in respect and fondness for this strangely learned and yet unpretentious man. He was a son of Canon Hugh Haweis, a notable London preacher and musical rebel (who had been lampooned by *Punch* for introducing Wagner's music into Anglican churches). The family name went back to the fifteenth-century poet, Stephen Hawes. Lionel, after public school at Marlborough and failure to hang on to a good journalist's job in London or to make good in Ceylon, wandered to Vancouver, tried to be a commercial photographer, and was now following what proved to be his last occupation. He lived with his wife, formerly his model, and a strikingly beautiful daughter, in a cottage crammed with books, paintings and *objets d'art* from the world's four corners, and particularly from what is now Sri Lanka. When our club tired of each other's work, there was always Lionel with something new and something old of his own, and stories behind all of them. During those two years I remember him reading us not only a novel, the "true history of Sindbad the Sailor", and more West Coast legends and "little lanterns," but most of seven long plays embracing the stories of both the *Ramayana* and the *Mahabharata*. From him poured a never-finished, unfinishable medley of learning and whimsy, gentle humour and philosophy, that ended only with his death in 1942. Very little of it was ever published, except by the act of Ganesha, but I've never ceased being grateful to Lionel Haweis for teaching me both the pleasures of creative fellowship and the importance of trying.

I emerged in the spring of '25 prepared to look once more for a summer job, but this time one came looking for me. I had been appointed editor-in-chief of student publications, and became noticed by downtown journalists. I took the most lucrative among the offers and became managing editor of a municipal weekly, the *Point Grey Gazette*. An old horizon was reappearing; perhaps I would end up a journalist after all. It certainly looked a faster way to security, marriage and the like, than the long years stretching ahead before the Ph.D. in EngLit.

I soon found, however, that journalism with the *Gazette* was minimal; what was maximal was selling advertising space. I was a one-man paper. Its owner was also the Reeve of the Municipality, too busy to do anything but write one semi-literate editorial a week to keep the paper headed down the Tory straightaway. I did everything else. I covered the weekly meetings of the Municipal Council and filled page one with

17

a shout-by-shout account of the proceedings of that operatic body (where my boss, as elected Reeve, was Pooh-Bah). Space I couldn't sell in the other seven pages I filled either with "boiler plate" (jokes, puzzles, recipes, world statistics, and like oddities supplied by an American agency) or with Social News (clips from the downtown press involving Point Grey residents), or items from the police blotter. The more ads, of course, the less I had to fill (though often I wrote the ads too) and the bigger my commission beyond salary. During an advertising lull I dug out my rejected short stories for Sedgewick's seminar, had them fed through our linotype, and ran them under pseudonyms. I enjoyed seeing them in print, lousy as they were — a harmless pleasure, as I never discovered anyone who had read them, or read anything else in the paper, except the Council reports and the bargain ads.

This peace was broken, however, by a sudden crime wave in the rich burgherish heart of the *Gazette*'s own municipality. Rape, murder, kidnapping. Every day now I shuttled between the Point Grey police desk and the Scottish Society's office (it was a Scots housemaid who'd been murdered) and my Reeve-Boss's chambers. I was making sure I got the scoop when our Police Chief and our Sergeant-Detective found the murderer, who had guiltily disappeared. But one day the downtown papers headlined the arrest of both the Police Chief and his Sergeant-Detective and the President of the Scottish Society. They were charged with kidnapping and torturing the murderer, who it was obvious wasn't the murderer at all, but a poor beaten-up Chinese houseboy somebody had been trying to frame. There was a long preliminary hearing, with top B.C. lawyers on each side. I got a front-row reporter seat — wow! — but so did every daily man, and since the *Gazette* came out only once a week I never scooped anybody with anything. The court decided there was no evidence to bring the accused to trial. Most of the reporters were sure they knew the murderer's identity, somebody socially top-layer and rich enough to buy a frame-up, but nobody ever named him. The Chinese houseboy promptly disappeared again, this time permanently; the rumoured murderer-rapist, some said, had committed suicide. By then I was back into English Honours, quite certain that whatever I was going to be it wasn't a newspaperman. The best I could do now, to salve my bruised pride, was to avoid being caught clueless as editor of the *Ubyssey*; and to make those First Class Honours. I just managed it.

During my final undergrad year the world of CanLit intruded only twice into our groves of academe. Bliss Carman, billed by the Canadian Authors' Association as "one of Canada's laureate poets", appeared on a balmy morning in autumn. He was on a quick tour of the West between his usual summering in the Catskills and his usual winterings in Connecticut. It appeared he hadn't visited Canada or written about it in thirteen years, for reasons not given. I had already formed the opinion, from Carman's anthologized poems, that he was nobody's laureate.

Consequently I did not leap for joy when I was called into the Head's office from the *Ubyssey* an hour before Carman's reading was to begin, and told by the great Doc that the Poet of the Open Road wanted someone to guide him into "one of our woodland trails", for a walk before his performance. "And that someone," said Sedgewick, impaling me with ice-blue eyes, "is you, sir." I argued I had a class. "I have already excused you." I argued I had an editorial to write. He regarded me silently and raised one eyebrow. I argued that every trail into the nearby woods either doubled back or petered out into piles of bulldozed stumps. Sedgewick merely waved at the window. "Be off, Birney. Canadian minstrelsy is waiting for you." I looked out. On a weedy plot that we hoped would someday be a lawn, a tall figure stood alone. He was gazing up at our usual cloudy sky from under what looked like a crumpled stetson. He was bundled in a long overcoat and tangled in a white scarf. I had heard it was his first time in B.C., and remember wondering if he had thought we were near tundra.

He acknowledged my self-introduction with a nod and explained he wanted merely "to be set going on a good nature path, and then left alone." I tried to explain UBC had just moved a few months before and the campus was still being carved from the woods. There was brush piled on undergrowth. But Carman was already striding ahead towards the first visible opening in some balsam, scarf streaming like a ship's wake. When I caught up with him at the trail's opening he insisted I return, that he never lost his sense of direction, and would be back in time for his reading. I warned him there were multiple forks ahead, the trail led nowhere, and he should lay arrow-marks with sticks on the path. He gave me a glance of pity that could only have been born out of total ignorance of B.C. undergrowth, and strode off.

He didn't reappear, of course, though when I found him — he'd left no trail-marks but hadn't gone far — he seemed annoyed. "I was about to return," he said, "but you are early." He was sitting on a stump where the trail branched into three thin tracks. I told him his audience had been waiting now for fifteen minutes. "Perhaps your watch stopped?" "O, I go by the sun," he said, looking up vaguely at the still murky sky. We came back without further conversation.

I was still prepared to enjoy his reading — at least there was a good timbre to his voice — but I found his accent artificial, with a New England overlay, and his platform manner pompous and condescending. I remember telling myself he was at least better than MacDonald and that I should concentrate on the poems. But even "Low Tide on Grand Pré" sounded slick and verbose, the way he read it, and "Hack and Hew" a humourless sermon. Worse, I now knew enough Victorian poetry to detect a steady echoing of Arnold, Morris and Tennyson in nearly all his verse. At least he didn't block the exits.

The other CanLit star flashing over our campus that autumn was Carman's cousin, the then still un-knighted Charles G.D. Roberts. He too had been away from Canada for many years, had been in England when World War One began, had enlisted in the British Army, and after the Armistice joined Carman in the United States. Roberts was also on his first reading tour of the Canadian West, and he too was rated a Canadian laureate by the CAA. A Vancouver paper had recently published a photo of him outside the CPR's luxury hotel in Banff, talking with the Chief of the local Stonies. Chief Walking Buffalo is on horseback; he is wearing an eagle headdress and beaded chaps. The Bard is on foot; he wears a Christie-stiff, a black eye-ribbon and a wing collar.

Since I had kept a warmer feeling about Roberts, from my schoolboy pleasure in his animal stories, I went to his reading in at least a neutral state. Among his anthology pieces I had taken a moderate liking for his "Potato Harvest". But hearing him read it now, along with many verses new to me, I decided Roberts dealt with cliché emotions and conventional thoughts. He was a good craftsman, and yet as dependent as Carman on outmoded rhythms and, even for details of Canadian nature, on nineteenth-century British phrasings.

Who was there alive and young and coming up, then? Would there ever be anyone to write the Canadian poetry that waited in the air? There was that man with the plain, even comic, name of Pratt, but I'd heard nothing more of him, and he wasn't even a Canadian. (Newfoundland was still a British Crown Colony. And I was unaware that a *Witches' Brew* had just been published in London.)

Consequently, when I was asked to give a paper to the Letters Club on a living Canadian poet of my choice, I decided on Roberts. I read everything of his available in the U.B.C. library, and came up with the essay whose conclusion follows.

It makes no mention of the puzzlement I felt, at the time, that the English Department had evidently sponsored Roberts' reading on the campus, with Sedgewick in the chair. How could my mentor and culture-hero, my own Matthew Arnold, preside over such exhibitions of second-rate verse as Roberts, Carman, MacDonald had served up to the students? In my undergraduate naivety I later made some remark about it to Sedgewick. He rounded on me with a great show of rage, calling me a snob and an idiot. These poets were not Shakespeares, he admitted, but they were among the best we seemed to have. They had been willing to ride the train out to this wasteland and read their best work to rascals like me without charge, though they themselves were so poor they had to reside in the United States to make a living. The least this University could do, since it paid them nothing, was to give them campus hospitality and a tolerant hearing. And if we didn't, by God, Sedgewick intoned in mock fear, there would be such storms brewing in the teacups of the University Women's Club and the local branch of the Authors' Association, and in all the other haunts of the patriotic *literati*, as would blow away all hope of further donations to the Building Fund, wipe out department grants and prizes, and generally shipwreck the whole Faculty of Arts.

The next year, when Roberts was again on the U.B.C. campus, Sedgewick wrote me in a different mood, though to the same conclusion:

> Charles G.D. Roberts lectures thrice this week on Canadian Literature & Wild Life. (The latter topic will neglect many aspects of the subject matter familiar to Roberts.) It is ungracious to say it, but I don't feel like entertaining him just now — and damn it all, I do find his verse stiffish (most of it that is), his novels insipid, & his animal stories sentimental. But like Enobarbus, I must be your considerate stone. God must surely be very lenient with hypocrisy.

Sedgewick will not go down in any man's memory as a hypocrite. But he was a realist. He and his students must use nothing less than the touchstones of Matthew Arnold to test the great world's literature; but Sedgewick was also a Canadian committed to Canada, and to what was still a small and impoverished college in a society intent on primary accumulations on the edge of nowhere. Though its literary coinage was fool's gold, he would pass it on with charming aplomb if by such gestures he could retain in his own Department of English Literature the gold standard of Harvard.

21

1926

The Half-Canadian Poet, Charles G.D. Roberts

Unpublished essay, University of British Columbia, February 1926.

Charles G.D. Roberts may have a prominent and even permanent place in our national verse but this doesn't guarantee him even standing room in world poetry. Why? Because he is imitative. The natural beauties of Canada are real enough, and different enough, from English and even American scenes to merit different forms and phrasings in expressing them. Roberts — and for that matter all the other Canadian poets — still fail to use the words that mirror their experiences; instead they echo the diction and verse patterns of Keats (*Orion*) and Browning. Browning himself, it's true, began with imitations of Keats, but he developed into being Browning. Roberts went on to mimic Tennyson (*Actaeon*) and Longfellow. He has shown some native ability in his verse to combine forthrightness with melodic grace but the talent dissipates in a maze of imported shrubbery. In his fiction, fake characters walk in stiff and borrowed dress.

His *Songs of the Common Day* are more original, but even the most popular poem in that collection, "Potato Harvest", ends in archaism and dated Turnerish landscaping:

> . . .Down the dusk hillside
> Lumbers the wain; and day fades out like smoke.

There is nothing uniquely New Brunswickian here. "The Sower" begins well, at least the landscape is Canadian, but it ends in Victorian cliché and sentimental moralizing:

> This plodding churl grows great in his employ.
> Godlike, he makes provision for mankind.

"Heal All" and "The Unsleeping" are robust enough but they too speak through borrowed tongues and see through others' eyes. The result is philosophical insincerity. At one moment he is rejoicing with Wordsworth at the contentment nature can bring man; the next he is lamenting with Emerson that "unassuaged desire" is fundamental to the universe.

22

In 1898 Roberts turned, with his *New York Nocturnes*, to cities for his subject. The scenes are undoubtedly ones he witnessed yet he describes them chiefly in the style of Rossetti (as for example "In the Crowd"). We are left not admiring the cleverness of a disciple but repelled by the timidity of a talented artist afraid to free himself from cramped metres and stale language.

The Book of the Rose is different, but mainly in the substitution of Swinburne and Kipling for his earlier masters (e.g. "The Stranded Ship"). In general, what might have been robust, even passionate, became merely sentimental.

His latest volume (*New Poems*, 1919) shows Roberts moving now into Darwinian themes and a more mature impressionism but the modes he has turned to are already established. Roberts sings of a pioneer land but he is no pioneer. Passions he may have but they are never allowed to grip and twist his speech into authentically *personal* expression. He has no voice.

It is an old colonial story. It seems that a land which has grown up in conformity, not out of rebellion, can only with great difficulty produce artists able to break from the conventional. Canada surely can give birth to great artists but it will not bear with them. They leave, and we are left with un-Canadian voices.

As I Remember
1926-1937

For the summer after graduation I swore off literature and went housepainting again, this time with my father, whose health was failing. In September, with a letter from the University of Toronto in my pocket assuring me of a $500 scholarship to last me through till May '27, I rode a CPR daycoach to unknown Ontario. I had chosen to work primarily in earlier English literature but elected also to take Professor Pelham Edgar's seminar in "The Modern Novel." Though Edgar included no Canadian in this course, his main emphasis being on Henry James, I began to realize, from after-class talk with him, that he was quietly devoted to the encouragement of any young writers who came within his ken. Occasionally he would invite me to have lunch with him at his old redstone home on St. George Street. On one of these socializings I met an ex-student of his, Raymond Knister; Edgar had already told me he thought Knister was the most promising young Canadian writer he knew, and lent me some copies of the American magazine *Midland*, with some remarkable realistic poems of farm life by Knister, and a very mature and craftsmanly short story.

Though all this made me anxious to know him, and I was assured that Knister was interested in meeting me, the encounter proved a flop. Knister, a rather gnarled little man looking older than his twenty-eight years, stuttered so badly he managed to finish only two or three sentences in the course of lunch; one could only witness in sympathetic anguish his struggle to speak from a mind bursting with desires to communicate. Afterwards Edgar told me that Knister, when alone with him, would have surprising periods of fluency. It seems that he wrote at a prodigious rate. It was fright at meeting a stranger which had tied his tongue with me.

I was amazed that Pelham, despite his status in the academic world and as an executive in the Royal Society of Canada, had been unable so far to interest any Canadian editors in publishing a Knister book. A few of his carefully-wrought imagistic poems had appeared in the *Canadian Forum*; otherwise he had been printed only in British or American journals. He was, Edgar said, working now on what would be an important novel — (this was probably *White Narcissus*, which appeared in 1929 and was largely ignored, or panned for its amateurish structure). I remember suggesting to Edgar that Knister, who was a bachelor, perhaps needed a wife to help him. "Ah," said Pelham, "I think he has one in mind, but she's even shyer than he." The following

24

spring I heard that Knister had indeed married — and gone to live in the States. When I next came to Toronto, in the fall of '32, I learned that Raymond Knister had drowned a few months before.

There were other young writers emerging in '27 with fates more fortunate, but I did not become aware of them then, nor can I remember even hearing that winter of A.J.M. Smith, Frank Scott, Abraham Klein, and the *McGill Fortnightly Review*, all dynamically alive in the next city to the east, during those eight months that I was immersed in Chaucer, Milton, Drummond of Hawthornden and the English-American novelists.

I missed even Lionel Stevenson's *Appraisals of Canadian Literature*, which had appeared in '26, the first book to take account of my own generation's writers. Ironically, I read the book and met its author only when I had left Canada, in the autumn of '27, and come to Berkeley on a teaching fellowship offered me by the University of California. (Toronto's English Department had as yet neither money nor courses to help a student beyond the M.A.). Stevenson, a Sedgewick pupil himself, had a deceptively soft, almost ladylike manner which concealed great acuity and toughness of judgement, and prodigious scholarly energy. I agree with Reg Watters that he was our best critic of CanLit till the appearance of E.K. Brown. Like Brown's, Stevenson's retreat to American universities and early death prevented much more substantial contributions to the building of a better Canadian literature.

The Depression descended in '29. My fellowship terminated, with my thesis only begun. I was lucky to find an instructorship at the University of Utah, but by the spring of '32 the budget cuts had made my lay-off there too almost a probability. In Canada in '32 I could see nothing ahead but another summer at U.B.C. and a $750-a-year fellowship back in Toronto for the coming winter. I took them, and returned to walk under the great elms of St. George Street.

I was now belatedly turning into a political animal. Utah had given me a year's leave of absence, but along with it the warning I'd be dropped for certain, a year after I returned there, unless the Depression lifted. That paralysis, however, was getting worse — there, here, everywhere. I could expect, by June '34, to join other young professors in a Bennett Relief Camp. I began reading Cole, John Strachey, and the political articles in the *Canadian Forum*.

I was still a Canadian but so occupied with my Chaucer thesis and the seminars in linguistics I had almost forgotten there was such a thing as CanLit. But I was occasionally scribbling satiric verses, stimulated by the companionship of two other graduate students in English, Alf Bailey and Roy Daniells. The three of us would lunch together once a week, joined sometimes by Robert Finch, a Fellow in the French Department who had just returned from study at the Sorbonne. I was impressed by the poetic talents of all three, though I argued against their preoccupation with traditional forms. It happened I had been the marker of Daniells' essays when he was a second-year student at a U.B.C. Summer Session, and I already knew he was loaded with both critical and creative ability. It was the former that gradually won out in his life, as in Bailey's, though I had not given up hope, until his death last year, that Roy Daniells might produce a major creative work.

Finch, of whom I talk later in this book, had an even wider range of artistic talent, for he was musician and painter as well as poet; but he too chose to remain an academic. His published poems have continued to adhere to the high standards of the craft he set himself, as did Daniells'. Indeed their sonnets are as fine as any written in Canada since Lampman. But they were cramped by the forms they chose. (Perhaps they will be the bright stars in an anthology of my generation, when and if the sonnet is restored to fashion, but I think that is an unlikely event).

Bailey had already published two chapbooks and was, beneath a modest almost timid manner, the most adventurous technician of us all. Finch had published only in the journals but, apart from the *Forum*, which they said was overstocked, and *Saturday Night*, which wanted Names and insouciance, there seemed to be no Canadian outlets for what they were now writing. The *McGill Fortnightly* had gone into permanent night; the *University of Toronto Quarterly* never printed poetry, only people writing about it; *Queen's Quarterly* took Queen's poets; *Dalhousie Review* Dalhousie's. One could always join the Canadian Authors' Association, of course, and write imitations of Carman or Roberts, and be trumpeted in the various house-organs of the CAA.

But by this time we grad students had gone through temporary discipleship to the Metaphysicals and the later Yeats and the early Eliot, and were diverging variously, — Finch into Valery (and, I think, Leger), Bailey deep in Jung and theories of history and post-Fraser anthropology, Daniells reading Rilke and Stefan George and, for reasons disturbingly vague, *Mein Kampf*. I was into Joyce and Breton and Dadaism, wavering between "philosophical" anarchism and social democracy. What passed for CanLit seemed remoter than ever from the contemporary realities of Canada and the world. A.J.M. Smith (still unmet by most of us) had written what had seemed the definitive epitaph on the "Maple Leaf School", in a *Canadian Forum* back in 1928, and yet the tree and its tinted plastic leaves seemed taller than ever and still running too sweet a syrup.

By January I had launched on a crash program of "leftwing" reading, starting with the *Communist Manifesto* and moving further into Marx, Engels, Kautsky, Plekhanov, Lenin, Stalin, with side glances into the literature of the new (Canadian) League for Social Reconstruction. At the home of one of its founders, the sociology professor Harry Cassidy, I met Ken Johnstone. He eventually became a successful Canadian journalist but he was at that time an active and informed leader of the Trotskyist youth of Toronto. To the same "evening" came Dorothy Livesay, whose *Green Pitcher* I had seen, thin lyrics showing at least imagist influence, but not much "social awareness". I learned she was just back from the Sorbonne, had a new book coming out, and a social-work job. It quickly developed that she was also a sentimental "fellow-traveler" of the Stalinists. Johnstone and I at once locked horns with Livesay over the role of the German Communist Party in Germany. I had been shocked to learn, from Stanley Ryerson and other young Communist Leaguers on the campus, that the Comintern had denounced all German socialists as "social-fascists" and refused a united front with their leaders against Hitler. I felt this refusal was the chief reason for Hitler's success, and was delighted to find at last, in Johnstone and his beautiful sister, two informed and clear-thinking minds able to expose Stalin's policies as not only tactically disastrous, as I thought, but basically unMarxist, Bonapartist not Leninist. That night began my conscious involvement in "the class struggle", and a seven-year loyalty to the cause of reforming the Third International or building a new one.

Meantime, I still had to find a living. I'd invested too much of my life in academic training to make it anything but foolish to drop out now; so courses still absorbed my weekdays, but the weekends were given over to working-class meetings, rallies, demonstrations, and to reading both Trotsky's *History of the Russian Revolution* and the unexpurgated *Complete Works* of Lenin. There was a night, at some Victoria College student debate, when I was almost diverted back to my earlier skepticism about human affairs by the arguments of a cherubic yet very intelligent undergraduate who was quoting Friedell and other historians I had not even heard of. His name was Norrie Frye. But I was by nature the optimistic sort of revolutionary and decided to cast my dice with the creator of the Red Army, and his brilliant Canadian supporter, the Toronto lawyer Maurice Spector. The founding secretary of the Communist Party of Canada, he had been expelled with Trotsky when Stalin emasculated the Third International.

In May '33 I returned to summer teaching at U.B.C., and to evenings given up to meetings, talks to socialist clubs, and the organizing of study groups for unemployed youths. I met only one Canadian writer during that summer, A.M. Stephen. I was already familiar with his collection of sentimental ditties (including much of his own) which he had published in '28 as *The Golden Treasury of Canadian Verse*. Now he was a left-winger too, but the sort who wanted to found his own party, and meantime try to lead everybody else's. The workers I knew thought him condescending and too fond of himself. We soon parted company.

The last winter in Utah went quickly. I arrived to be reminded it was indeed my last. Having nothing to lose but my gowns, I became a political activist, founded a Marxist student club on the Mormon campus, and led an investigating committee of faculty and students into a martial law area where striking coal miners were suffering mass arrest and beatings. By June '34 I was well-enough known in American Trotskyist circles to be invited to New York to work on the party's theoretical organ, the *New International*. My wage would be $15 a week, and the promise of a winter overcoat. Melodramatically, the day before I was to hop the bus to Union Square, I got a cable from dear Pelham Edgar in Toronto. Unasked, he had somehow wangled a $1500 Royal Society fellowship, making it possible for me to complete my thesis at the University of London. I accepted joyfully.

I made the money last for a year and a half, returning to Canada early in '36. In Toronto I presented my completed thesis and passed the orals, whereupon I was given a doctor's hood and a lecturer's job at the bottom of the English Department's ladder in University College.

That summer I taught again at U.B.C., and so did E.J. Pratt. We got to know each other at last, and formed a warm and enduring friendship. Back on the Toronto campus in September, I was at once hard at work preparing lectures in advanced courses, with little time to give either to CanLit or CanPolitics; but by November I found myself involved once more in both. I was approached by the *Canadian Forum* to be its Literary Editor.

"We feel that the literary side of the paper has not been properly developed," Professor George Grube, its Reviews Editor, wrote me. His board wanted more and, if possible, better stories, poems, literary articles, etc., and he wanted me to hunt for them. Contributors, however, were not paid, nor were the editors. Nor was there an "editor-in-chief". "The policy of this paper is decided by the board as a whole, of which of course you would be a member."

I would have preferred moonlighting for money, since I had now both a wife and a smaller salary than before I gained the Ph.D. — but I was flattered. The *Forum* had a sixteen-year reputation as Canada's kind of *New Statesman*, a truly literate social-democratic monthly. Its contributing editors included prominent members of the League for Social Reconstruction and of the CCF (which it helped to launch) such as Eugene Forsey (Senator-to-be), King Gordon ("Ralph Connor" 's son), the sociologist Leonard Marsh, and the poet Leo Kennedy. On the board itself I would have as colleagues, in addition to Grube, Eric Havelock, who like Grube was a classical scholar at the University of Toronto; Frank Underhill, professor of Canadian history (Political Editor); Frank Scott, McGill's remarkable professor of Law; Pegi Nichol, the Toronto painter (Art Editor); Graham Spry and Eleanor Godfrey.

I was particularly drawn to the chance of developing the literary side of a magazine which had already attracted work from Pratt, Smith, and Finch as well as from such editors as Leo Kennedy and Frank Scott. And I could see also there would be opportunities to apply Marxist aesthetics to contemporary literature. It was of course well-known in university circles now that I was of the Trotskyist persuasion, while the other editors were parliamentary socialists, but Frank Underhill was shrewd and informed enough to know that as a Trotskyist I did not accept the Stalinist notion that a piece of writing was better *because* it was written by a "proletarian" or even by virtue of its being about one. This was the aesthetic now being propagated in Toronto's *New Masses* by student "Marxists". The *Forum* was willing to tolerate me as an ally against their "lumpenproletarian" hostility. Underhill and I agreed that I should have freedom to apply my own concepts of "historical materialism" to the literature I discussed; on the other hand, if I wanted to engage in essentially *political* controversy, I must use other outlets. In consequence, the *Forum*'s political articles remained Underhillian; mine were published under pseudonyms in the American *New International*. Meanwhile, for my Canadian comrades, I wrote theses about tactics, leaflets, and the like; and for my academic advancement, Chaucerian articles published in the "learned journals".

The first issue in which I had a hand (December 1936) carried Pratt's "The Dictator", an A.J.M. Smith poem, and a salty Juvenalian satire by Louis Mackay. Louis and I were now fellow-instructors in the UC cloisters and soon good friends. Until his departure for Berkeley, he remained the *Forum*'s wittiest and most intelligent humourist. These three poets, however, together with Klein and W.W.E. Ross (some of whose poems I had ready for later issues), were already *Forum* contributors; I needed new ones, both from Canada and abroad. In the first months of 1937 I was lucky enough to give first publication to poems by men of international standing. With the help of an old friend of the *Forum*, Professor Barker Fairley, we secured a long and important poem by C.M. Grieve ("Hugh McDiarmid"), sent me from a tiny island in remote Shetland; and direct from the Loyalist lines in Spain I received a moving lyric, signed by the Canadian doctor, Norman Bethune.

Poetry, however, because it was generally shorter than anything else, had sometimes to be treated as filler. When seven or eight of us sat around Eleanor Godfrey's diningroom table, making up the dummy far into the night, there would be a cry from her or from Mark Farrell, the business manager, for something between ten-to-fifteen lines to fill out a column. Twice I had nothing to offer except two recent verses of my own. One of these, "Slug in Woods", was noticed by Ralph Gustafson, who had been sent the issue because his *Alfred the*

Great was being reviewed in it. Gustafson, out of *bonhomie* perhaps for a favourable notice, wrote asking to include my "Slug", vintage 1928, in his *Pelican Anthology of Canadian Poetry*. That was the beginning of a long friendship whose first fruits, before I had even met him, was his free and steady submission of excellent poems to the magazine, and my first recognition as a "maker".

Since George Grube was faithfully passing to me any of the review-books he regarded as literary, I had also to increase the roster of *Forum* reviewers, or swamp the magazine with my own notices. My university colleagues loyally helped me, notably E.K. Brown, Northrop Frye, Norman Endicott, Herbert Davis (in English), and Gilbert Norwood, the Classics Head (who used to lampoon us all with instant limericks, while waiting for his tea in the Faculty round-room at UC). Friends too helped. I thumb an old *Forum* file and see "W. Judson", a young lawyer and poker companion. He served for twenty years, a Justice of the Supreme Court of Canada. As this goes to press I learn sadly of his death.

Review-articles were naturally my own province, though I was also securing essays from American contacts I had already made, such as V.F. Calverton, Sherwood Anderson and James T. Farrell. My own "first" was a re-appraisal of Housman, in the January '37 issue. I was gratified when it prompted a fan letter from one of the editors of Macmillan, Toronto. Other kind words filtered in to me as the year wore on, both from academics and from CCF-ers; I was all the more deflated, therefore, when in September the Head of Macmillan, Hugh Eayrs, wrote Grube cutting off the *Forum*'s book-supply because of his personal displeasure with one of my notices. I reprint it here not because I think it is a very good review but to document the nature of Toronto's literary establishment in 1937. I was unfortunately unaware, when I wrote the review, that the author I was accusing of being out of touch with Canadian life was still confined to a wheel-chair. Later, when we met in Victoria, Miss Audrey Brown forgave me most generously and kindly for what must have come to her at the time as cruel insensitivity. We agreed to disagree on the quality of her poetry and on my critical insight. It was also evident that she was her own woman and no complacent captive of the CAA. It was her publisher, however, who never forgave, and who seemed determined, indeed eager, to punish that socialist rag, the *Forum*, not for blundering into insulting his author, but for daring to criticize the Canadian Authors' Association.

1937

Moon-wist in Canadian Poesie

Review of A.A. Brown's *The Tree of Resurrection; Canadian Forum,* August 1937.

In 1931, from the collective forehead of Victorian poesy, sprang Miss Audrey Alexandra Brown, fully-armed with the plaudits of the Canadian Authors' Association and its attendant ladies. The fact that Miss Brown's early conventual education and invalidism had led her into verses "lost in a dream of opal-amber days", bearing no visible relation to the western Canadian coal-town in which she lived, or to this world, was accepted not as a natural limitation but as a romantic testimony to the purity of her genius. A rather notable absence of originality in thought or phrasing was explained as the blessed visitation of the "classical spirit" to Nanaimo. And those clamorous echoings in her verse of the nineteenth-century Great were welcomed as "traditionalism", as proof that even in its new greatness Canadian literature, like Canadian politics, condescended to remain loyal to the Empire. That it was now nothing more than condescension was indicated by the writer of a prize essay in the *Canadian Bookman* (Feb., 1935) who pointed out that Miss Brown's "Laodamia" was not only "the most valuable contribution that has yet been made to our national literature" but also a poem to equal anything to be found in all the tomes of Keats, Shelley, Browning or Tennyson.

However just may be this parallel, what seems to have been forgotten is that Keats and the other boys beat Miss Brown to publication by a few score years. One is reminded of these harsh chronological verities by a new volume of Miss Brown's poems, especially since half of it is a reprint of the verses by which the lady arose to Canadian fame, and the rest is the same star-dust and dawn-glow and dreams, tuned to the sweet sharp thin pluckings of a zither. (Here the reviewer is lured into the traditionalism of Miss Brown.)

So far as there is any development beyond the 1934 volume, it consists in some pruning of this scented lushness — but not enough, not enough — and a deepening of religious feeling. The title poem, somewhat diffusely Tennysonian, asserts a faith in personal physical immortality. There are other verses assuring us that beauty dies, but death is kinder than life, and God exists. There are more antimacassar embroiderings on Greek legends, and "delicate raptures, fragile

31

ecstasies" upon Nature. The forests of British Columbia continue to yield for Miss Brown daffodils and no dogwood, halcyons not woodpeckers, innumerable oreads but never a logger. Like her Nadya Cyrilovna, Miss Brown may properly lament

> I am tranced, I am drowned
> In music of nightingales.

Of the forty-two poems, only one mentions so local and ephemeral a being as a coal miner; he is a naughty fellow, who is punished for his amorousness by a creepy supernatural death in a folksy sort of mine. The one other incursion into the world of the flesh is a warning to the Spanish that if they go on killing each other they won't be able to "build the fair creation their wiser fathers willed" — whatever that means. Elsewhere Miss Brown speaks of war only in terms of silver trumpets and gold adornings.

There is no doubt that Miss Brown has been, for some time, the most decorative and melodic of our younger writers, and she has not lost her virtuosity. When she can steady her movement with the sincerity of a personal emotion, as apparently in "Past Noon, October", she achieves a tender and poignant lyricism. But even here the bookish veil between the author and her ragged unclassical environment is never quite parted. None of the new poems succeeds as well as the earlier, frankly romantic "Laodamia", here reprinted. Beneath its monotonously silken rhythms and legendary petticoats there move at least some dignity and pathos.

Most of the new poems are in fact definitely inferior to Miss Brown's first work. They continue to evoke little more than pale memories of more and more poets — Coleridge and the Rossettis, Housman, Yeats, Arnold, Milton, Sidney, St. Francis, Brooke — and where in this anthology is Miss Brown?...

For those who are not bothered by pastiche, Miss Brown will no doubt continue to co-star with Shelley. The author herself seems to feel considerable confidence in her future:

> I never had a garden. All my flowers
> Art of dim amber and dream amethyst
> And twilight-rose — rainbows and stars and mist —
> Too delicately fair for sun or showers...
> But they will blossom still when June is gone.

Brave words — but there is usually a frosty December ahead for young writers who remain as contented with their juvenilia as were their first provincial admirers.

As I Remember
1938 - 1939

Heavy teaching loads and growing political involvements kept me from any serious attempts to write verse myself during the next two years. I hoped instead to find new poetry for the *Forum*'s literary columns from my University College students. There was — there always is — plenty of talent but most of its possessors were already traumatized by the academicians. Any students intending a career as university teachers of literature were fenced off as freshmen from the vulgar Pass People into the four-year course called English Honours. Survivors of that were then steered into M.A. and then exported for Ph.D. programs, just as I had been.

There were a few exceptions. Miriam Dworkin, in my "second-year-pass-English," avoided Honours, made social work her profession, and steadily rose to national prominence as a poet. She married another poet, Patrick Waddington, a CBC newsman of great charm and all-round writing ability; but in his short life and often straightened circumstances Pat found time from journalism to write only a few poems (some of which I published in the *Forum* or the *Canadian Poetry Magazine*) and a half-dozen short stories. These were the days before the Canada Council.

Among undergraduate honour students of mine who survived the English Department's straitjacket to become creative citizens I think especially of Mavor Moore, already a man-of-the-theatre, as befitted the son of Dora Mavor Moore. He wrote a properly bawdy short story for my Chaucer seminars, and I ghosted a play-prologue for his mother. Later we would collaborate on my first radio drama when we were colleagues in the CBC's International Service. He is today Chairman of the Canada Council. Then there were the wisecracking twins of my short-story seminar: Johnny Weingarten, who wrote a *Varsity* column under the name of Wiregarters, and gave me an essay on Eighteenth-century Jest Books, and his inseparable straight-man, Frankie Schuster; they were famous, for me, before even the Army Show or Ed Sullivan's radio programme, or the Wayne & Schuster of CBC-TV. There was no way, however, I could wheedle them on to the *Forum* staff.

It was more established writers, of course, whom I came to count on for a regular supply of poetry. In the late Thirties I was able to provide the initial outlet for many of Abraham Klein's poems, especially on the Spanish Civil War; Pratt's "Submarine" and other pieces; A.J.M. Smith's "The Archer" and "The Bridegroom"; as well as poems by authors then virtually unknown, such as Anne Marriott (whose first chapbook, *The Wind Our Enemy*, was about to appear), and the teen-aged Raymond Souster.

Ray and I didn't meet until after the War but we corresponded frequently. Though I thought some of his adolescent work sentimental and formless, I had to return many acceptable manuscripts simply for lack of space. In 1939 he wrote me: "I know I am sending you too much... but I feel trapped... as far as publishing goes and the *Forum* is the only place I can turn to.... Can you suggest a few openings I don't know about?" I couldn't, not Canadian ones. He wasn't writing the rhymed Victoriana required in the thirties by the *Canadian Poetry Magazine* and the quarterlies of Queen's and Dalhousie (Toronto's refused anything not looking like prose). Souster's wonderfully suggestive style was too bald for them, and too North American for a British journal. His passionate directness, his satiric edge, his celebration of ordinary sensuous pleasures, were lost on the academics. Though his milieu was the streets and the humbler citizens of Toronto, I could only advise him to try American outlets or start his own magazine. He did both with some success, co-editing *Direction* while serving in the RCAF and publishing in U.S. journals. It was Ronald Hambleton, however, another youth whom I came to know in '39, who brought Souster's work into book circulation with his *Unit of Five* (1944).

Most of my hours as a literary editor were spent reading unbelievable doggerel from all parts of the country, written by persons with more leisure than talent, considerable self-regard and no critical sense. I still keep a food-stained missive from a regularly-rejected young Canadian in England. It begins: "Dear Earl Brinnley... you boys have not treated me any to well" and demands I give reasons for refusing his drivel. I sent them, whereupon he wrote me on hospital stationery that my attitude had brought on "an attack of tuberculesis". I understand, however, that he is still alive and well in London and printing his own poster poems.

There were consoling pleasures. One was the challenge of finding readable tales when there was no money to pay for them. Sometimes I would even manage to beg something from Morley Callaghan or Hugh Garner, and there was the satisfaction of seeing stories I had published listed in E.J. O'Brien's annual *Best Short Stories* along with famous Americans. Three out of every four items so listed in his Canadian section between 1937 and 1940 had, in fact, appeared in the *Forum*.

In a search for still more fiction I initiated in 1939 a "first national Canadian short-story contest". Morley and Bertram Brooker agreed to join me in judging, and I found a donor willing to put up a fifty-dollar prize. It went to Louella (Mrs. Donald) Creighton, with an honourable mention for John R. Fisher. Several runners-up gave us enough publishable stories for a year or so ahead. Most of the entries, however, were of value only to morbid sociologists studying Canadian colonialism: amateur imitations of *Macleans'* formula-romances; redcoat heroes in the northland; fictionalized tracts on the relation of God to Social Credit. In a report on the contest, published in the *Forum* (Oct. 1939), I wrote: "There may be little difference in the rural idioms and idiocies of British Columbians and Nova Scotians, but there certainly are distinctions in their traditions and in their natural scenery. These mutations, vital in any literature, were especially ignored by the dozen who for their theme chose love, whether sacred or profane (it was mainly the latter). Lurve may be the same the whole world over, but it is surely the business of the story-writer to make it seem just a little different each time. The young hobo who blossoms with pure passion for a hobelle in a box-car on a Winnipeg siding ought to betray at least some overtones of character which would distinguish him from the dying biologist 'purused' by a middle-aged nurse in an Egyptian hospital. But in the stories I have in mind their personalities were interchangeable. The only phenomenon which may be definitely Canadian about the love-stories was that in most of them the female was unquestionably the hunter. This may have a relation to the surplus of women in our population or merely to the fact that a surplus of the love tales — and a high proportion of all the entries — were written by women.

"The bulk of the stories were predictably proletarian, focussed on strikes, the disintegrating effects of unemployment, or fatal accidents to workers. There were a dozen studies of exploited toilers, ranging from teachers and bank clerks to Great Lakes sailors, domestic servants, farmwives, delivery boys, and bootleggers' assistants. There was even a somewhat satiric study of a Quebec unit of the Communist Party.

"Such entries made up most of the best submitted, and also most of the worst. A number of eloquent attacks on capitalism had to be quickly, even if regretfully, discarded because although they told stories they did not tell them about recognizable human beings. It is quite within the bounds of the short story to present homeless unemployed lads who, through little fault of their own, come to death beneath the wheels of freight trains. Indeed, the fact that three stories had that identical theme is testimony to the awareness of the Canadian amateur writer to the more symbolic tragedies of our day. But to be a proletarian artist it is not enough to voice the protests of workers; it is necessary to *be* an artist, to shape material painstakingly into an illusion of life. One contestant allowed his dying freight-hopper to gaze at his dismembered stumps, from which the blood poured like fountains, while calmly and lengthily reviewing the economic causes, the slump in the prices of agricultural products, etc., which led to his dismemberment.

"Such pamphleteers, like many earnest left-wingers, have curious ways of insulting the working class. They make the fight for socialism seem much easier than it is: a hard-bitten young factory boss is suddenly converted into granting wage-increases and a general good time to his employees when he learns that his father is one of the strike leaders, and that his poor old mother has died. It might happen, but ninety-nine per cent of strikes are not won so accidentally, and to ignore that fact takes away, somehow, from the heroism of the workers' struggle. Then there are those who seem to think that the lower classes should be written about only in words of not more than five letters (including as many damns as will fit in), with a careful absence of anything unusual in phrasing and anything usual in punctuation or spelling. There is a notion that a class-conscious carpenter must be physically a burly orang-utang and at the same time an instant interpreter of Marx's theories of surplus value and an intuitive wielder of the Dialectic. Such writers are, perhaps, not sharp enough Marxists to realize there is nothing too good for the worker, who should not be written down to any more than he should be written up to, and that it is surely the business of proletarian literature to make, out of the half-realized emotions and incoherent thoughts of workers, some clear, coherent and moving representation of their lives."

It was what some booksellers call the "non-fiction prose" which was the easiest to find, and most *Forum* subscribers expected. Indeed the editorial columns may have been the most read. Though anonymous, most were known to be written by Frank Underhill, whose acerbic and laconic style shone through. Witty, ironic, an expert on Canadian political history, with a courageous, almost devil-may-care approach to national politics, this Toronto University professor was probably the most formidable socialist in Canada. Inevitably he was thoroughly disliked by the influential business men among the University's Regents, and when the War came, his job hung by a hair. I admired him and he was jovially tolerant of me at first, though reputed to be as tough on anyone to the left of him as he was to the bourgeoisie.

I think, in the longer run, it was the *Forum's* ample book-reviewing service that gained us the widest readership. The notices were signed, and so were seen to be written largely by readers of more than local reputation in their field. I recall only one occasion in which a pseudonym was used, and it was the result of a hoax engineered by our brightest literary reviewer, Louis MacKay, the young lecturer in Classics who wrote Juvenalian verse satires for us and for *Saturday Night*. There was also a writer of rural lyrics living down in Niagara country who had recently published a chapbook of them under the title *Viper's Bugloss*, the Linnaean name for an oddly handsome Ontario weed. His name was John Smalacombe. When his modest booklet came to the office for review Louis asked for it, saying he had been

36

"following this chap's stuff." When Louis brought me his notice I thought it less than kind, but I hadn't yet read the poems and the review was witty enough to use. A week after it appeared, the *Forum* got a badly typed letter with a smalltown postmark from John Smalacombe enclosing a furious but well-expressed rebuttal of MacKay's review, and demanding equal space for it. When I showed it to Louis, he rubbed his hands gleefully. I must run it, he said, but could he have an inch or two for rebuttal of the rebuttal? Didn't the *Forum* need literary controversy? the good old dialectic? etc. So our next issue contained both Smalacombe's blast and MacKay's even louder counterblast. Promptly came another letter from Smalacombe, which, the shrewd fellow pointed out in his cover-note, would take up merely the exact column-space of my stupid reviewer's attempt to argue. Belatedly I smelled a rat. Louis' own zany style and editorial knowhow were not this time quite concealed. I confronted him with my suspicions, he confessed, and John Smalacombe disappeared permanently from the roster of Canadian poets. It was a pity, really, but we did have a reputation for socialist honesty we needed to keep up.

We were, in fact, maintaining a monthly review of new Canadian and foreign literature ampler, more varied, and almost as sophisticated as that of our only rival in this field, *Saturday Night* (which had, in Mary Lowry Ross, a reviewer of *New Yorker* quality). Morley Callaghan couldn't afford to give his stories away but he was willing when approached to write an occasional critical article for us, as was Sherwood Anderson, and American critics such as V.F. Calverton and Edward Maisel; and we had a "stable" of thirty or more Canadian reviewers scattered across the country.

My lengthier appearances in the *Forum* were chiefly devoted to contemporary "foreign" authors — the Americans Faulkner, Farrell, Anderson; the English Housman, Huxley, Day-Lewis; the London journals, *New Writing* and *Horizon*. However, it had been agreed when I joined the *Forum* that I would write a regular tabulation of world news, in the Dos Passos manner, presented without commentary, but selected and arranged with an eye to the contradictions of capitalist society. This appeared monthly from January 1937 under the pseudonym Rufus and titled "Another Month". In April, when I ran an extra "Rufus" report on the facts behind the Guelph Reformatory riot, Frank Underhill expressed anxiety that the *Forum* was publishing "Trotskyite" views. I offered to resign but a compromise was reached: Eleanor Godfrey became the Editor, Mark Farrell, the new business editor, took over the column as "Rufus II" — actually continuing it in the same spirit as mine — and I promised to stay within my literary boundary.

By this time, indeed, there were bonds of friendship and mutual esteem linking the editorial staff, and a common enjoyment of the experiences of producing something at least vaguely like a Canadian *New Statesman*. *Forum* editors and their spouses had become (along with some Toronto contributors, CCF supporters and critics) a social group of a naturally shifting but always lively nature. It was in this context that I formed friendly and admiring relationships with Morley and Loretta Callaghan; with David Wyke (at that time the sole black doctor practicing in Toronto) and his wife, Marguerite (who was later to be the only woman Senator of the short-lived West Indian Confederation); with Norrie and Helen Frye; with the wonderfully humourous Mary Lowry Ross, and Eustace, her wise but over-modest husband. He seemed almost reluctant to admit that he was both the University's astronomer and the W.W.E. Ross who had published, in the *Forum* of the Twenties, the first Canadian imagist poetry. (He was rediscovered by Colombo and Souster in the Sixties.) Among the unifying figures in this heterogeneous society was a social worker — my witty and politically courageous wife, Esther — and Margaret Reid Richardson, a biologist, CCF stalwart and discriminating reader of every *Forum* issue. "Maggie" was a Wife of Bath figure of Falstaffian proportions and capacity for enjoyment, an omnivorous reader, and possessor of a large house whose doors were open to us all.

If there was an equivalent Tory literary society in Toronto in the Thirties, I never heard of it. There were many highly literate and able Liberals, indeed, and some of them no doubt had a social focus around B.K. Sandwell, *Saturday Night's* prestigious and formidable editor. A dapper man of polished manners but aggressive wit, he was a natural essayist and an excellent judge, shrewd and flexible within the limits of his kind of Liberalism. He helped me re-establish some confidence in my country's ability to realize itself without losing the best in both the British and the American cultural traditions (though he would not have given the latter equal status in parenthood). I would have liked him less, of course, if he hadn't liked my work and been the first to pay me for a poem — ten dollars, equal to a week's rental of our Hazelton flat.

Occasionally I met other Canadian writers by virtue of being a Toronto English instructor. One was a solemn gruff fellow who stalked into the Department's cloisters direct from his Simcoe farm one afternoon. At that time he was known as Frederick Philip Grove. I had long been an admirer of *Over Prairie Trails*, the best description of midwest winters I'd ever read, but his *Two Generations*, which I had recently slogged through, had put me off. I thought its techniques heavyhanded and oldfashioned, and his attitudes as humourless, morose and egoistic as he now seemed in person. He had evidently decided he was now the Canadian Master of Language and in consequence should be given a position in University College's English Department. I never knew why he thought we were to be the lucky ones. Perhaps E.K. Brown reviewed his new book favourably, or had simply written suggesting he drop in for tea at the college next time he was in Toronto. At any rate, tea he had, a full departmental one in the round Chapter Room, with the Department, all eight of us, in dutiful attendance. As he became more outspokenly demanding to be our ninth, and more paranoid from our gentlemanly Principal's attempts to change the subject, the socializing rapidly deteriorated, and Grove marched away in the direction of Victoria College without the Special Lectureship he had decided to accept.

A very different and welcome writer did join our staff, though briefly, shortly after Grove's sudden manifestation. This was Douglas Le Pan, fresh from Oxford, a modest youth of great amiability and obviously high endowment, but with a blocking stammer that seemed to hold down his natural liveliness, and made some senior professors mutter that he would never last as a college lecturer. The stammer faded, however, as Douglas went on to Harvard, and into the War, and out to be, among other things, Principal of our College and one of our most respected authors.

During the spring of 1939 Hugh Eayrs' feud with the *Forum* was renewed, no doubt through a tactical blunder of mine. Macmillan, as the Canadian distributor of James Joyce's *Finnegan's Wake*, sent the *Forum* a review copy. Grube, the Review Editor, handed it to me, since I was indeed a Joycean fan and had recently given a one-hour public lecture, under University of Toronto auspices, on Joyce's life and writings. I was delighted at the opportunity to read at last this *magnum opus*, of which I had seen only the small fragments already published in European journals. And I was pleased that I would have as my reward a copy of a coveted volume I could not afford to buy. However, Macmillan were demanding that our review appear in the next issue. This might have left me seven days to read and review a thousand-page work of the densest sort of layered prose, but there was also a pile of spring exam papers on my desk which had absolute priority. I got the exams marked and managed to rush to the printers a short impression of the *Wake*, with the statement that it was the first book I had ever reviewed without reading more than a sixth of it, and if this displeased the publishers they could have it back. Eayrs had his secretary phone the *Forum* at once demanding *Finnegan's* return, and I mailed it off. Eayrs, however, still not appeased, ordered that review copies never again be sent to the *Forum* so long as I was on its staff. Whereupon my co-editors met and agreed to refuse all books from Macmillan. Happily, once more Ellen Elliott quietly made peace. She was influenced perhaps by the unanimous support given me by *Forum* colleagues but also, I should think, by the fact that the *Forum*'s circulation, though small, was national and probably included all the people likely to buy *Finnegan's Wake*.

It was a teapot tempest, but the arrogant interference of a basically uncultured book-merchandiser with the normal freedom of the press shocked the civil libertarians on the *Forum* Board into solidarity with their lone Marxist-Leninist, on this issue at least. For us all, Eayrs' blackballing gestures were symbolic wavelets reaching Canada from the widening storm of authoritarianism in Europe.

Within months the storm was world-wide and our government had clapped sail and was steering into it. By Orders-in-Council Ottawa declared us into the Second World War, and Parliament quickly passed a War Measures Act making prison sentences mandatory for speaking or publishing any opinion likely to hinder the prosecution of the war. During that winter, most Canadians thought it only a Phony War. "Our side", the fat democratic cats, howled hideously from fencetops, watching the fascist dogs join to hunt and destroy one by one the little rabbit countries. It was all as the Trotskyists had predicted, and our Toronto spokesman was already in Don Jail for six months for saying so, and no voice risking print in his defense. In the Canadian press now the professional war-lovers had free run. In literature Kiplingitis was revived; the verse columns blossomed with jingoism. There was only one way to ridicule these warmongering scribblers, and that was to greet them with the savage smile of irony. In that mood I wrote, for the *Forum*, "To Arms with Canadian Poetry". Forty years later I've found it necessary to warn young readers that, as Artemus Ward used to put it, "this was writ sarcastic".

1940

To Arms with Canadian Poetry!

Canadian Forum, January 1940.

Now that we have collected the more obvious enemy aliens behind barbed wire, clapped the soapboxers and anti-war pamphleteers in jail, and threatened the pacifist parsons with the same medicine, is it not high time we turned our attention to the poets? The body of our loyal citizenry, pre-occupied with the new mass production of airplanes and sox, is plainly unaware that sedition is rife on the home verse front. We should not lull ourselves with the argument that no one reads Canadian poetry, for the fact remains that metrical propaganda is being regularly *exposed* to the public eye. Moreover, whatever the war aims of our government, some of this verse is not in keeping with them. Worst of all, the most serious offenders are precisely those poets who are said to have some reputation among the intelligentsia. Who knows but that their utterances might become known beyond the borders of our country, and prejudice His Majesty's relations with foreign powers?

Certain exceptions may happily be made at the start. Mr. Nathaniel Benson has left no doubt of his patriotism in a stirring appeal entitled "A Canadian to America!" which appears in the current (October) issue of the *Canadian Poetry Magazine*. Mr. Benson justly pictures the distressed shades of Lincoln and Washington sneering at the failure of the United States to enter the war on our side. "Arise, America!" he concludes, "Arise, America, and strike!"

But what of Sir Charles G.D. Roberts, Wilson McDonald, and other senior bards? We have heard nothing from them since the war began. In such days as these may not silence be treasonable? Nor will we be fobbed off with wedges of geese in the northern sky or the lisping of unbombed Canadian children. The time has come when nature is not enough.

Some of our leading journals likewise remain in a most disturbing rhythmical lethargy. The post-peace issues of the *Dalhousie Review* and *Canadian Homes and Gardens* contain not one measured line which might conceivably be said to bear upon the present struggle. The October *Queen's Quarterly* presents but a single poem, "The Old Eagle", by E.J. Pratt. Although this makes a to-do about an airplane, the craft is obviously of a simple commercial type without bombing equipment. In the last *Canadian Forum*, it is true, Dr. Pratt has printed a long composition which makes suitably unflattering references to Hitler, but the ditty seems to eschew the time-honoured phrases and images of patriotic poetry, and shows a dangerous tendency to treat war as in itself a bad thing. . . .

The Canadian Home Journal has not, I'm sorry to say, done much better, with the exception of "A Mother's Prayer" by Faye Gould McLean, which contains at least three satisfying lines:

> He came, a soldier, through my door.
> "I've joined," he called, "they've said I can.
> Gee, Mum, I really am a man!"

The ending, however, which I forbear quoting, unfortunately emphasizes a certain reluctance in the Mother to recognize the automatic manhood of her nineteen-year-old soldier son.

One is happy to record that at least one Canadian periodical is giving space to the poets who fully understand their duty. In the Toronto *Saturday Night*, Mr. J.E. Middleton publishes a well-merited "Protest" against those who "when Hell is loose again . . . prate learnedly of Peace!" The first phrase is perhaps a bit unfortunate, since our scald has not clearly confined the boundaries of Hell to enemy territory, but Mr. Middleton clarifies his vision in the following week's issue of the same journal, by an elegy in memory of the missing seamen of H.M.S. Courageous. They are pictured marching up the "golden way" and receiving a blessing from the wounded hand of Christ himself. This satisfactorily establishes the partisanship of Heaven in the present war and helps to re-establish that grand tradition of piety which made all the Canadian poetry of 1914-1918 forever memorable. Mr. William Patterson of Calgary manages in the same issue to combine a similar reference to the Saviour with an ingenious appeal for recruiting:

> My Work of Mystery . . .
> Ye thought it done; 'Tis but begun.
> Now, who will follow me?

How inspiring to think of our noble volunteers, the First Canadian Division in England, being under the personal command of Major-General Christ Himself!

I regret to note, however, that *Saturday Night* has on at least one occasion allowed versifiers of a different stripe to intrude upon its space. I refer to an affair rather cheekily called "For the Duration", by one Joyce Marshall. It reads, in part,

I'll never pen / A martial ditty
High in bombast, / Low in pity...
I'll never urge / The lads I know
To go where I / Need never go.

This sort of thing may perhaps not actually discourage recruiting but I should think it might be likely to prejudice discipline in His Majesty's Forces (always supposing that it would be likely to fall into Their Hands), and so actionable under the Defence of Canada Regulations.

It is with a genuine relief, therefore, that one turns to the beloved and traditional poetry-corners of our daily newspapers. It is true that even here not all editors have yet learned to discriminate. From September on, the Toronto *Daily Star* has continued to print unseasonable trifles about autumn colouring and love and the like. There is as yet nothing in the War Measures Act which deals with such writings; yet if this example were to be followed by all our poets, would not the effect be definitely to cause disaffection to His Majesty and even perchance to interfere with the efficient prosecution of the war?

To the credit of the rest of Canada, let it be said at once that the apathy of the *Toronto Star* is being daily repudiated by Vancouver's loyal *Province* and the monumental *Montreal Gazette*. I wish there were space here to quote at length the inspiring "Highlander's Hymn of Hate" and the "Lament for the Passing of the Kilts" which have appeared in the Sunday supplement of the former. I must content myself, however, with but fragmentary reference to the rich out-pourings of melodious patriotism which have steadily graced the editorial page of Montreal's bulwark of our press.

The first days were of course the most difficult for the *Gazette*, as for all of us. For some reason best known to the fickle muse, there was a gap of almost two weeks between Britain's declaration of war and the appearance of Canadian poetry properly adjusted to the event. (I cannot help but feel that all this is connected with Mr. King's lamentable slowness in declaring Canada herself at war.) But where other editors resorted to their files for rhymes plainly written in what might now be called the disloyal days of peace, the *Gazette's* literary helmsman ingeniously reprinted the glorious calls to battle issued by Rudyard Kipling and other alert Englishmen in the parallel days of 1914.

By September 18th, however, a Canadian poet had leaped into the breach, with a dithyramb in celebration of two "great captains" of the past. Mr. Alan MacLachlan, writing during the unfortunate days when our Allied Command seemed to be hesitating before the Westwall, aptly reminded the Empire that Conde and Turenne "waited for no German to make the first attack." On September 20th there followed a beautiful lyric by an old patriot, Vox Populi, entitled "Floreat Anglia

Atque Gallia." With that fine triumph over logic which gives the poet his peculiar power, Populi declaimed:

> Canada's a peaceful land.
> But shall Canada stand aloof when she hears
> the loud-mouthed guns?

The answer was, of course, No.

No event has been too great or too small to be shirked in celebration by the *Gazette's* gallant soldiers of the quill. Mr. Richard Callan, of St. Lambert, P.Q., taunted the Reds for their pact with Russia ("Nazi champagne healed the sore"), and Miss Eunice T. Holbrook Ruel, following carefully our Allied positions, saw

> Over the forts of Saarbrucken
> The great Archangels wing and watch
> As once in Bethlehem.

Mr. W.J. King, who had made a fine individual sally against the Huns by describing them, in a "September Ode", as "creatures from the jungle", returned to active service in November with "The Crusade." The Germans are now revealed to be prehistoric saurians, and the poet ends finely: "Once more the dragons fear the cry 'St. George!'"

Even Armistice Day, a theme presenting peculiar difficulties for our battling Pindars, was not overlooked. Fittingly, it was the Honorary National Vice-President of the Imperial Order of the Daughters of the Empire who stepped into the breach. "Mayhap," she suggests, "the poppies e'en lift an accusing head." But "avaunt such thoughts",

> And though the very fiends in hell should laugh,
> With choicest flowers pile we high the Cenotaph
> And pledge anew our swords to this now holy war.

Another poetess — and it is indeed gratifying how the women of our Dominion have sat typewriter to typewriter with the men in this important work of the home defence — apologizes most charmingly for fellow poets who have not yet fired their poetic rounds at the hated Boche:

> It seems to me there's so much happening
> That poets haven't got time to write.
> Like the white dove of peace on muted wing
> They watch for rays from heaven to give them light.
> But is there darkness in this war for right?

The answer, of course, is again, No.

In such a veritable Maginot line, such a fortified Parnassus, as the *Gazette's* bards have built and held, it is difficult to single out any one poetic pill-box for especial praise. Were I forced, I should, however, name the clarion ode to "Poland" which appeared on November 17th. Although its author, Mr. Wheaton Bradish, subscribes himself "An English Visitor to loyal Canada", I think it well to quote from him here — I wish I could say *in extenso* — as a shining mark at which our Dominion troubadours may shoot. The poet sees our fair young nation flying to Britannia's aid,

> The bloody tyrant's will to foil
> And force the forsworn fiend's recoil.
> The scions of Montcalm and of Wolfe
> Will chase with zest the foul werewolf;
> Two races in such keen rivalry
> To slay such noisome devilry. . . .
> The flaming fiery-cross hand on
> Until it gilds Pacific's bourn. . . .
> Escorning Nazi savagery,
> Ah! hearken to Britannia's cry:
> Poland dies not, without I, too,
> Death's portals with her journey through!

In these accomplished couplets there is immediately evident the alliterative heritage of our doughty Anglo-Saxon (as distinguished from Low Saxon) forebears, together with those bold inversions, audacities of metaphor and unusual twists of word which convince us at once that Mr. Bradish is of Shakespeare's land. Gaze, finally, at the couplet with which the visiting scop hails our Dominion:

> Unflinching in two holy wars
> Unstinting in old Britain's cause.

In the surprising triumph of that rhyme there surely speak not only the indomitable spirits but also the authentic accents of the true-born Englishman.

We need more Wheaton Bradishes. The time is rapidly approaching when we shall be forced, in the interests of an enduring peace, to curb the verse-hoarders, discipline the shirking sunset-fellows, instruct our willing but inexperienced Kiplings, and intern the seditious peace-rhymers. A Poetry Control Board is on the order of the day and I hope that our government will have the perspicacity to recall Mr. Bradish to act as its Controller. It is on such poetry as his that our Empire rests.

1940

Before 1940 was over, however, the war had become real for the British too, and almost real for a whole division of Canadian troops in England. The *Forum* didn't change much. Its permanent financial crisis continued; its editorials remained mildly socialist; its newsprint deteriorated. Thanks to the reluctance of censors to read poetry, I was able to present definitely anti-imperialist-War opinions through the work of Ralph Gustafson, and mildly pacifist feelings from Alf Bailey and Floris McLaren. Publishers became warier than ever, of course, and there was even a reluctance on the part of the Ryerson Press to send us a review copy of Anne Marriott's *The Wind our Enemy*, until Lorne Pierce decided that we, at least, were not the real enemy. The writers themselves, even those outside the jingo pack, too often seemed willing to censor themselves. One such used the phrase "Nazi munitions lords" in verses he sent me. The rest of the poem was passable but I wrote him I wouldn't use it unless he found a less hackneyed phrase or at least deleted "Nazi"; did he think the Allies were using only Krupp shells? He replied that he was indeed glad if I would run the phrase without "Nazi" but he had not known "whether such universal application would be censorable in Canada." Some poets have the hearts of hamsters.

Still, it was the bards whose hearts thumped the bravest who wrote the worst, and deserved to be derided. When the Ontario Library Association invited me to give them a lecture on "Humour, Old and New" I took advantage of the occasion to include a *Forum* review that I had just written to blast a book the Toronto stores were busily puffing. It was the script of a BBC show called *Alice in Blunderland*, advertised as "the most popular radio skit yet produced in wartime"; most verses in it were doggerel of this calibre:

> How doth the Nazi crocodile
> Improve his Lebensraum
> By teaching Germans how to heil
> In all lands that allow 'em.

The whole book was an insult to the memory of Lewis Carroll and a betrayal of the spirit of comedy. Real humourists, I said, are never whole-hearted patriots. "They are either internationalists or anarchists and they go to jail or their deaths daily now in Germany, in Italy, in Russia. And they may also in Canada, even if we win the war, unless we distinguish wit from caterwauling, and elect real humourists to office. The real problem is how to get humourists to run." The lecture was not a success.

Public lecturing, reviewing, editing, made up only one of a half-dozen lives I was living in the beginning months of the war. My bread-and-butter profession was still teaching university students. A third, which would eventually replace it, was free-lance writing. And there was that fourth life, which had begun in 1932, of a Marxist-Leninist. In that category I wrote political essays under pseudonyms for New York journals, and manifestoes, leaflets, programs and speeches for a Canadian organization which the War Measures Act had now driven underground.

By mid-1940, however, I decided that this war of capitalist powers had become also a necessary struggle to prevent the world becoming totally fascist. Another Armageddon, but one in which I was willynilly involved. My wife was Jewish, and pregnant with what would be my Jewish child; I had a stake in Hitler's defeat. With the U.S. still holding aloof, and France in collapse, Britain and its Commonwealth provided the only military counter. Stalin's Russia, which had made a pact with Hitler and had invaded Finland on the pretext of self-defense, was plainly no longer the workers' state Trotsky still believed it to be. It could not be relied on to defend Jews or to preserve any of the liberties that made life for me worth living. I dropped from the Marxist-Leninists and prepared to join the "war effort" in whatever way I could.

For a while, however, the war did not seem to want my efforts, and I went on with my three other lives. On a summer trip to Vancouver to see my mother, I made a try, through CCF circles, to find new writers, as well as subscribers, for the *Forum*. I got only three fresh contributors: Paul Halley, Carol Coates and William McConnell. The last-named was writing promising fiction, both short and long, which no one else wanted to publish. I thought for a time that he would develop into a professional fiction writer, but Bill liked to eat regularly, and had other talents more marketable. After a spell in the army he "went in for law", and is now a practising attorney.

Certainly there was no visible "west coast scene" in Vancouver in 1940. Lionel Haweis was still alive but fragile and writing little. Dorothy Livesay had retired at least temporarily into marriage and childbearing. The only active Canadian *littérateur* I saw in British Columbia that summer was Lionel Stevenson, whom I had known in my Berkeley days. He was now a professor in the University of Southern California, a man with an established reputation (in the U.S.A.) as a scholar of Victorian literature. I summoned the nerve to show him some verses I had been working at, and was pleased by his careful, helpful reading of them. Stevenson's encouragement, added to that already given me by Ned Pratt and Louis MacKay, made me resolve to work towards a book of poems. Ned soon backed his judgements by including some of my shorter pieces in the *Canadian Poetry Magazine*, which he was now editing. It was the willingness of those established figures, at the top of their own abilities, to find time to encourage unknown beginners such as I still was, that prompted me in turn to initiate, the following year, the first "creative writing" class to be offered by the University of Toronto (the first, probably, to appear anywhere in Canada), and to continue with such efforts throughout my teaching life.

Back in Toronto that fall, with nothing more to report for the War Effort than a rejection from the Navy (too old at 36), I joined the University Training Corps as a private-cadet. Since the daily infantry training had to be sandwiched in between lectures and seminars in four undergraduate and two graduate courses, I reluctantly but finally resigned my *Forum* editorship. Loyalties remained, however, and the need to write. The *Forum* alone in Canada provided monthly space for rational comment on the war-bedevilled literary scene, and I was happy to contribute reviews and articles. Frank Underhill, who had neither said nor published anything contrary to the War Measures Act, was continuing steadfastly in his socialist criticism of the ambiguous and shadowy policies of MacKenzie King's government. This was enough now to sting various members of Toronto University's Board of Governors into a serious attempt to have him fired. All of us who knew Underhill and had worked with him joined in a counter-rally which ultimately preserved his living, and incidentally broadened public awareness of the need for "eternal vigilance" to maintain the liberties of the *Canadian Forum*.

Ralph Gustafson: Neglected Canadian Poet

(Review of *Poems*, eight poems offprinted from the April number of the *Sewanee Review; Canadian Forum*, August 1940).

It is good to see an American journal of the distinction of the *Sewanee Review* giving Mr. Gustafson such deserved space. The first poem, in lyrical-dramatic form, is the weakest, the diction lacking dramatic variety and the format too abrupt and disjointed, but the other seven rank with the best of his work. His particular vein is a philosophic use of nature imagery, usually in short and highly concentrated lines. In a letter to this reviewer recently Mr. Gustafson described his technique as, in part, an "attempt... to make sensuous imagery fuse — come simultaneously, as sensations do when experienced, a series of parallels rather than hyphens...." When successful, this method produces sharp and imaginative writing somewhat like that of Edith Sitwell's, but less precious and more reflective. The dangers, which Mr. Gustafson does not always avoid, are obscurity and cacophony. The present offprint shows a wise search for greater variety in rhythm and an increasing clarity without loss of concentration. "Toponymy" is especially good, and the Biblical rhythm of "Crisis." Mood and thought are authentic and wedded to our times, grim despair and reluctant acceptance of a world once more mad with slaughter.

(Review of *Epithalamium in Time of War; Canadian Forum*, October 1940).

Gustafson's latest poem is far superior to most written by Canadians these days, superior in freshness and concentration of imagery, maturity and boldness of vocabulary, and in awareness of contemporary thought and technique. It is occasioned, one infers, by the marriage of a sister to a young lieutenant, and the theme is the ancient and inexhaustible one of the world renewing itself in spite of horror and holocaust. There are nine stanzas each of eleven lines skillfully interrhymed and occasionally alliterated in a manner which shows the influence of Hopkins.

The rigours of the stanza-pattern lead at times to jerkiness in phrase and a squeezing of syntax, with consequent losses to rhythm and to clarity, and there is some straining after mere surprise in the image; but these are faults of the best poetry of our time, and are more endurable than the saccharine emptiness of the belated colonial Georgians who still pass for poets in Canada.

This is a privately printed chapbook of eleven pages, one hundred copies, none for sale. It is a pity Mr. Gustafson did not seek wider publication; but perhaps he did. What Canadian journal would publish a poem of ninety-nine lines, particularly one as contemporary in style as this? Only the *Canadian Forum,* and Mr. Gustafson did not, I believe, submit it here.

Canadian Poem of the Year

Review of Brébeuf and his Brethren; *Canadian Forum*, September 1940.

By turning inland to the eastern borders of Lake Huron and back in time to the 17th century tragedy of the martyred Jesuit mission among the Huron Indians, Mr. Pratt has shown once more that he can adventure successfully into ever new and difficult terrain. In this, his ninth volume, there is the same narrative verve and dramatic intensity, founded on a fine factual assimilation of his subject, which have helped to make him not only Canada's most remarkable poet but also the finest poet of the sea writing today in the English language. There is the same technical brilliance in the variable flow of sound and flexibility of line — here in a running blank verse, agreeably modulated by anapaests — and once more the imagery reveals, though in a more subdued fashion, his flashing imagination and his panoramic eye. Most important, the story of Brébeuf, Lalement, and the other pioneer priests tortured to death by the Iroquois, gives full scope for the human qualities of Ned Pratt, his unabashed warmth of heart, and his enthusiasm for mankind in its moments of courage, endurance, comradeship and self-sacrifice.

It was inevitable, of course, that the writing of a tragic epic about a Jesuit saint would impose sharp limitations, and it is one of the revealing things about Mr. Pratt, and about this Canada we live in, that it should have been written at all, let alone so well, by the son of a Methodist minister and a professor in a Methodist college. Yet the devoutest Catholic will surely read it with pleasure and certainly without offense, though he may find that the religious motivations and experiences of the Huron missionaries are at the best romantically and energetically apprehended rather than emotionally realized. The ties of understanding between the poet and his characters are not so bound in the heart as in *The Roosevelt and the Antinöe,* and the reader's blood is stirred less even though his sensibilities are more painfully wrought upon — as in the torture scenes.

The theme has forced the poet to mute two of his most individual qualities, his cosmic humour and his gusto. There is nothing here of the excellent foolery of *The Witches' Brew,* with its essential Pratt combination of hilarity and learning, or of the jovial rhyming and lusty imaginings of *The Titans.* Nor is there room for any of the satirical subtleties of *The Fable of the Goats* or the religious lyricism of *The Iron Door.*

On the other hand, there is a restraint and a simplicity which are comparatively new, though exhibited in many of Mr. Pratt's shorter poems since the first days of *Newfoundland Verse*. And there is, by the same token, an absence of those weaknesses which have flowed from the excess of strength in his previous narrative work. In *Brébeuf* the tempo never gets out of hand, the voice does not hoarsen from a too prolonged *fortissimo* (as at times in *The Titanic*), and there is none of the rhetorical fireworks which occasionally bedim even the best of his poems. Above all, in *Brébeuf*, bigness of deed and character is not made merely spectacular or grotesque, but is heightened into the grand.

Brébeuf is then in some respects Mr. Pratt's best work, though by no means illustrative of his manifold talents. It is not so well integrated as the *Roosevelt*, nor as individualized, nor as emotionally full. Its climax is more satisfactory though still, as in his other narratives, falling somewhat flat by being too intensely anticipated. But *Brébeuf* is eminently faithful to its heroic aim, which is to exalt a group of suffering and undaunted human beings against their background of medieval France and barbarian Huronia. No finer introduction both to early Canadian history and to contemporary Canadian poetry could be given school children of this country than Mr. Pratt's *Brébeuf*.

Writing in the *University of Toronto Quarterly* two years ago Mr. Pratt reminded critics that though there are no peaks in Canadian poetry there are at least a few foothills "and the mountains come to birth out of the foothills." With this volume Mr. Pratt's own achievement continues visibly to rise into what may be the first of our Rockies.

As I Remember
1941

My various lives became more eventful in 1941. I began getting my verse accepted in Toronto magazines, and in midsummer Dorothy Livesay wrote inviting me to contribute to a new journal founded on the West Coast, *Contemporary Verse*. Although I was not to meet its revered editor, Alan Crawley, till the War was over, we quickly began a correspondence and developed a friendship which remained until his death in 1975. Alan, although totally blind, "read" (by the voice of Jean, his devoted wife) every word of the constantly growing volume of mail that came to them from both Canadian and American poets, and sent replies discussing the submissions, whether or not he accepted them. His judgement was acute, his taste sensitive, his energy constant. In its ten years of life, his small multigraphed quarterly did more perhaps to advance the reputation of Canadian poetry than any other magazine before or since.

This was the year too in which I met A.J.M. Smith, whose work I had been publishing for several years now. He called on me when he came to Toronto looking for fresh writing to include in the first edition of what was to prove a very seminal anthology, his *Book of Canadian Poetry* (1943). I showed him some "western" poems, including my own as yet unpublished "David", which he took "on spec". Ned Pratt had one of his glorious stag-dinners for A.J.M., to which came, I think, E.K. Brown and Northrop Frye, perhaps A.S.P. Woodhouse, and probably Leonard Brockington. I still remember Art as the shy tousled fellow who kept running his hands abruptly with great sighs through his black hair — a man as complex as his poetry, baggy pants under neatly tailored coat, cigarette-holder rakish in his mouth, coldly glittering glasses concealing bright and passionate eyes. We had somewhat different approaches to poetry but became friends at once, a brotherly relationship I have treasured to this day. His inclusion of several of my poems in his Chicago book greatly extended my American audience, and made me see the importance of anthologies in the encouragement of younger writers.

Beginning back in 1940 and now through 1941 I had been trying without success to get my poem "David" into print. E.K. Brown, who liked it so much, later rejected it for the Toronto *Quarterly* and for his guest-edition of Chicago *Poetry*; Ellen Elliott, now the co-editor of Macmillan, accepted it with others of mine for a volume but then decided not to publish me till the war was over. Ned Pratt, who had made the approaches to Macmillan for me, was unwavering in thinking the poem ought to see print now, but he did not have the space for it in the *Canadian Poetry Magazine.* Art Smith and Ralph Gustafson had already included "David" in a jointly edited *Contemporary Canadian Writing,* but they could not find a publisher for their collection.

It was my old friend, the *Forum,* which agreed to find the three pages in their December 1941 issue. Its appearance prompted my former professor, Pelham Edgar, to recommend it to Lorne Pierce, editor of the Ryerson Press. The latter asked to see all the poems Macmillan had rejected, and published them (as *David & other poems*) the following year.

In 1941 I began also to add a millimetre or two to my academic status by publishing articles on Geoffrey Chaucer (for me to this day the greatest of narrative poets) in "learned" American journals. Coincidentally it was also the year I was at last elevated, after eleven years as a university instructor, to the rank of assistant professor; my salary was now two hundred dollars higher than I had started with.

My "war efforts" also showed some progress. After eight months of being drilled on the campus, and at a summer camp in Niagara, I graduated as a second-lieutenant and started in September another eight months of drilling more students.

At the same time I began the first Creative Writing "workshop" ever countenanced at the University of Toronto — and probably the first in Canada, except for the "Advanced Composition" class commenced in, I think, 1941 at McGill. Toronto's English departments, which had opposed my idea for four years, now allowed it on condition that the course run for a half-year only and be limited to Senior Honours English. I think there were eight in the workshop; three of the women became professional Toronto journalists (Janet Tupper, Anita Friedman, Jan Tyrrwhit) and a fourth, Mary Horton, is now an editor and publishing poet in England.

The Universality of Abraham Klein

Review of *Hath Not A Jew*, New York, 1940; *Canadian Forum*, February 1941.

Ludwig Lewisohn, in a preface to these poems, rejoices that "a young Montreal attorney was destined to be the first contributor of authentic Jewish poetry to the English language". Mr. Lewisohn does well to praise *Hath Not a Jew*, but he praises it for the wrong things. In polished and mordant satire, dancing wit, metrical versatility and originality of metaphor this is one of the finest volumes of verse ever written by a Canadian of whatever race. But it is where Mr. Klein is striving most to be "Jewish" that he is least poetical and most turgid. Having tried *Hath Not a Jew* on some of my friends tutored in an orthodox Schule, I find that much of Mr. Klein's obscurity is equally impenetrable to them.

All Jews and some Gentiles know, of course, that a Shadchan is a marriage broker, and will not miss the edged humour of Mr. Klein's poem of that name. Who but a Talmudic student, however, can enjoy a poem made up of lines like the following:

> The smiling Kahana; Shammai in a mope;
> Hillel instructing an obtuse Ethiop?

Even Eliot, who taught Mr. Klein tricks both good and bad, footnoted his "Waste Land". Unfortunately, it is necessary to wade through such obscurantism, not to speak of the arrogantly Israelitish preface by Mr. Lewisohn, to arrive at the real poetry of the volume — the writing which speaks to all men. . . .

He who persists will be rewarded. As readers of the *Forum* will know — Mr. Klein is an old contributor — he is a virtuoso in metres. His quatrains, in their fusion of musical neatness with surprising and moving imagery, remind one of Emily Dickinson. His sonnets are so skilfully wrought you do not notice they are sonnets, let alone Italian sonnets, and he is almost equally dextrous with terza rima, the prose song, and Eliotic free verse. Occasionally rhythm suffers for the sake of rhyme or figure, but the latter are so pungent and Chaucerian that it scarcely matters:

> He abhorred the tribe of Moses;
> Barbs in his heart were their hooked noses.

Satiric character portraits make up much of the volume; occasionally these are light to the point of nonsense verse, but more frequently they are edged in irony and bitterness, which is as often directed against his own race as against its oppressors. Here Mr. Klein's "authentic Jewish self", of which Mr. Lewisohn makes so much, has its authentic expression. Only the Jew really knows how to make jokes about Jews — and only he should. And none but the Jew can speak with proper passion of Israel's eternal sorrows:

> The wrath of the people is like foam and lather,
> Risen against us. Wherefore, Lord and why?...
> The sun rises and leaps the red horizon
> And like a bloodhound swoops across the sky.

For the woes of Jewry Abraham Klein has no counsel but endurance: "Plant small stones for eyes so that no tears may run." Zion in Palestine is still half-dream, and its consummation no panacea. The Messiah will not come except through a change in the hearts of all men, a change to enduring peace and social equality. Jerusalem must be builded here. There may be another world —

> But I will take a prong in hand and go
> over old graves and test their hollowness:
> be it the spirit or the dust I hoe
> only at doomsday's sunrise will I know.

1941

Pratt's *Dunkirk*

(Review) *Canadian Forum,* December 1941

Dr. Pratt's eleventh volume of verse, consisting simply of a poem of some three hundred and fifty lines on the rescue at Dunkirk, towers above the other narrative poems of the year in Canada, as *Brébeuf* overshadowed other poetry in this country last year. Not that "Dunkirk" is or pretends to be an epic; it has neither the length nor breadth of "Brébeuf", but wisely concentrates on the civilian heroics of the great withdrawal. No poet yet knows enough, nor can be detached enough, to write at this date of the event as a whole, and perhaps, under the War Measures Act, no Canadian as realistic as Pratt would be permitted; but within the limits of the space and the view, he has done a fine job. There are no cheap patriotics, no fuzzy political moralizing; instead, there is a re-creation of the peculiarly "British" mixture of bravery and almost ridiculous matter-of-factness, of instinctive seamanship and amateurishness, which made possible that strangest and grimmest of all boat-races.

The prolog pictures the "three hundred thousand on the beaches, their spirit-level straining west!", and the summons for their rescue sounding through England. Then follows "Regatta and Crew", a roll-call of the ancestors of these sea-going islanders, conducted with the author's characteristic gusto and dramatic verve. Like the men he celebrates Ned Pratt is one of the "lovers of the beef of language", and his lines race with the yachts or lag and plunge with the "dutch scoots and square-stemmed bawleys rank / With kelp, fish-scales, and the slime of eels...."

Compared with *Brébeuf* the new poem is not only shorter but more episodic, less a rounded and serene whole. Yet it has many of Pratt's virtues missing from that Jesuit epic of last year. There is some of the high spirits of *The Witches' Brew* and *Titans,* and there is what *Brébeuf* could scarcely have had: Pratt's peculiarly accurate and intense portrayal of the sea. The salt Atlantic has become, through him, a tenth province of Canadian literature, entered upon nearly twenty years ago with his *Newfoundland Verse* and now, under the tragic compulsion of the times, explored to the far reaches of the English Channel. Placed beside the memorable *Roosevelt and the Antinöe, Dunkirk* is less moving, more tentative, but it has the same unique fusion of pictorial originality, scholarly factualness, and heady speed. Finally, though *Dunkirk* is not so much a story as a story-that-can't-be-told, it is superior to all his previous verse in one important particular: poetic concentration. With the exception of the fourth section, there is scarcely a place where a line may be cut without the wound showing. The maimed version in the current issue of Chicago *Poetry* bleeds to high heaven. In the original there is scarcely a phrase which does not strengthen the poetic conception. The rhetoric of the "Cachalot" is here held in leash, without being, as in *Brébeuf*, silently muzzled. Pratt's great epic, fusing all his varied gifts and exploring a rich and indigenous theme, has not yet been written. But he has here made another step toward the writing of it.

This steady annual production of poetry of real consequence by a Canadian is now in danger of being too much taken for granted.... In England there is no one in narrative poetry now to touch him, as the briefest comparison with Masefield's poem on Dunkirk, "The Nine Days Wonder", will show. In America he stands only below the authors of *John Brown's Body* and *Conquistador*, and he has the power to exceed in originality the finest productions of Benet and MacLeish. May the gods of war give him the time, and the lords of peace the opportunity.

58

1942

Advice to Canadian Anthologists: Some Rude Reflections on Canadian Verse

A review of *Voices of Victory* published by Macmillan, Toronto, 1941 for the Canadian Authors' Association; *Canadian Forum*, February 1942.

In such a big country, our poets have long cultivated a very small potato, with almost no export value. Some apologists have unjustly blamed the soil, labour conditions, bad markets. The trouble seems to be rather in the growers, who have preferred to propagate from old and leathery seed-potatoes, inclined to gush forth a luxurious topgrowth, concealing sometimes no spuds at all.

Lately, the crop has been improving, with such stout hoe-ers as Pratt, the *quondam* Montreal group, and the westerners. Yet the product remains little known either inside or outside Canada.

One reason for this is surely the badness of our anthologies. Verse-collections are the minstrels' chief advertising media; they can combine the uses of a growers' guide and a Chamber of Commerce release... The Canadian pageant has generally been a grey one, pretentiously dull and bowdlerized, as with E.K. Broadus, or genteelly dull, as with the *Oxford Book of Canadian Verse*.

Better times are certainly ahead, now that two younger poets good enough to get published outside the country, A.J.M. Smith and Ralph Gustafson, are preparing anthologies, the former under a Guggenheim award, the latter for the Penguin publishers. And there have been welcome preludes, collections of recent verse, such as Ethel Bennett's *New Harvesting*, the "Montreal" group's *New Provinces*, and the special Canadian issue of the American magazine *Poetry* last April. Recently, however, another "treasury" has appeared which may profitably be discussed only as a model of how not to compose an anthology.

Its title, *Voices of Victory*, suggests the first Don't. No faithful anthologist will attempt to conscript poets around the "war effort" or any other effort. It not only raises false hopes of the utility of dactyls in repelling tanks, it can't be done. One of the two objectives of the tome is "to let the poetic genius of Canada and the Canadian people sound a spiritual challenge to the brutality of enemy despots and tyrants" (I quote from the modest little preface); yet, out of sixty-eight printed pieces, twenty-three ignore the despots and the whole war, while six others are plainly pacifist in implication. Moreover, the heretics, in the main, present better work, mainly because they know what they are writing about. The challenges to Axis brutality are hurled chiefly by ladies in cities several thousand miles from the bombings, or by gentlemen who owe part of their literary prestige to the fact that they are several decades older than any conceivable draft-age. With such, blood tends to be a crimson word in a line, not something they expect to shed, and one turns in haste and relief to the present poets of England, many of them men actually in the services, writing, when they have a moment, not so much about the bloodshedding as the meaning of it, and hoping beyond mere military victory to the victory of all men over the forces which set them at war.

If our patriotic bards had to smother an occasional incendiary, their readers would need to smother fewer yawns. Not that it is necessary to be a fighter to be a war-poet; but, lacking experience of the reality, one must at least throw out the mouldered imagery of lances and pennants, and put the imagination to work. To become furious at the Nazis simply because English children are killed in a war with them, is to be a rhyming journalist, not a poet; equally innocent Berlin babies have been killed by our bombers. You would scarcely suspect it possible, however, from *Voices of Victory*. Not a one of these voices knows how to "challenge" tyranny, because they have not learned that poetry challenges by thought as well as by sentiment, that a real poet thinks of the world a-borning, or that might or should be born, as well as of the grizzled and savage old era we live in. To our typical Canadian songster, however, thinking about anything, except springtime, is a new experience; he needs some basic training before pitching himself into the metrical battlefield. When the assault of modern democracy began in Spain was he not the same poet who spoke condescendingly of the "propagandist" who espoused the Loyalists? and who never imagined that poesy could concern itself with anything but maple leaves and the honk of geese?

It may be argued in the present case that however faint the Voices of Victory may be, the book is to be supported because its primary declared objective is "to contribute whatever the proceeds from its sales may be to the Canadian Red Cross British Bomb Victims' Fund". This brings us to the second Don't for the thesaurist. If you are seized with the passion to see yourself and your friends in print, be honest about it; don't use blitzed Londoners for an excuse. The fastest, most effective way to have helped such a cause would have been to forego the book and donate its publication cost — as well as the silver medal, the cash prizes, the teas, and the other expenses of the contests staged to get material for the compilation — directly to the Bomb Victims' fund. The fund would have more money, and Canadian song would be spared further unfortunate publicity.

The truth is that the "Poetry Group of the Toronto Branch of the Canadian Authors' Association", which fathered the enterprise, was driven by the not unnatural determination to see itself between covers. To make sure that it should, it not only ran a preliminary national competition for which its own members were eligible, but arranged a complicated plan so that any grouper who did not win one of the three awards or one of the twenty honourable-mentions might nevertheless be published among the Voices, and among the best of the Vocalists. The scheme involved a second division after the prize lyrics, made up of one verse from each of the "distinguished Canadian poets" invited to contribute, *and* one verse from each of the Toronto Group who had lost out in the competition. The whole of this section was then arranged alphabetically so that the reader could not tell, without consulting the list of the Olympians at the back, who was distinguished and who was a member of the Toronto Group.

The plan threatened to go haywire when the committee of judges who consented to select the best poem submitted by each member of the Group, for inclusion in the volume, threw out *all* the poems of nearly half the organized laureates as unworthy of publication. Some of the disappointed accepted the judges' decision; others managed somehow to appear, behind the judges' backs, with some of the faintest runes in the volume. I cite these sordid details not simply because, as one of the judges, I can vouch for them, but chiefly to show what happens when a chapbook is published not primarily for the good of literature, or even of war victims, but for personal publicity and parish-pump loyalties.

There is here another Don't for the arranger of lyrical pageants: avoid the group, any group; "flee fro the presse, and dwell with sothfastnesse." (Both Chaucer and this reviewer are ineligible for membership in any Canadian Poetry Society.)

And there is a related Don't: avoid claiming representativeness, even though you seek it. You will always miss someone whose fame will haunt you twenty years later. "Every distinguished Canadian poet is included", says the jacket, and the book lists them all in an afterword. But, missing from list and from *Voices*, are at least a dozen whose published work is well above the level set by the Choir. Where is Abraham Klein, whom Ludwig Lewisohn recently called "the first Jew to contribute authentic poetry to the literature of English speech"? Where is A.J.M. Smith, who last month won a famous international award, a Harriet Munro memorial Prize, for the best group of sonnets published in *Poetry* during 1941? Where are F.R. Scott and Robert Finch, important contributors to *New Provinces*? Where is Ralph Gustafson, another winner of more than Poetry Group prizes? Where are Louis MacKay, Anne Marriott, Floris McLaren? One answer is that, with a single exception, they are not in Toronto. Another is that Sir Charles G.D. Roberts hasn't got them on a list.

Finally, if you want to produce an album which will galvanize, not paralyze, coming Canadian scalds and their possible public, don't launch your little vessel on the wash of a competition. No matter how "discerning" your adjudicators, and how neatly you pick them to embrace the sprawling geography of our land, there will probably be at least one, as there must have been in this case, who not only fancies that a mediocre verse on a war theme is better than a good verse on any other theme, but is also unable to distinguish the hackneyed from the fresh. It is difficult otherwise to explain the choice of the fifty-dollar prize poem, where aptness of theme and sincerity of intention are countered by a language so dated and affected, so full of purple clichés, faery foam and nightingales and fragrant flowers along the riverain, that it is difficult to think of anyone in England let alone in Calgary, Alberta, writing it any time after the death of the seventh Edward. It could not have been preferred over the second and third prize verses (which are much and progressively better) on the ground of content, for these also are unimpeachably patriotic; it must have triumphed because one at least among the judges was voting for his schoolboy memories of Keats and Tennyson. . . .

As I Remember
1942 - 1945

Early in 1942 Arthur Smith wrote me that he had been talking to Whit Burnett, editor of *Story* magazine, the most prestigious short-fiction journal in North America, and that Burnett, learning I gave the only graduate course in Canada on the history of the short-story (from the Egyptians to Faulkner), wanted me to find eight to a dozen unpublished writers north of the border to make up the major part of a special Canadian issue. He would pay $25 to $35 a story. Smith was already at work collecting a poetry section, to which he would write a preface, and I would prepare a short history of the Canadian story. I was still a great innocent about literary business, and naively happy to be the instrument for bringing Canada's active fiction writers before *Story*'s public. I wrote my consent to Burnett and to Smith at once. Between January and May what spare time I had over from teaching and drilling and baby-tending went into a search for stories.

I sent out fifty letters, choosing a range of authors from such established figures as Leacock and MacLennan down to the best of the young *Forum* writers. I soon had a half-dozen good new pieces, including stories by Sinclair Ross, the prairie novelist; Sybil Hutchinson, a talented graduate student of mine; William McConnell; and one of Emily Carr's "Klee Wyck" stories Ira Dilworth had persuaded her to send me; and the promise of stories to come from Morley Callaghan, Hugh MacLennan, Dorothy Livesay, Ralph Gustafson, and several others. (Grove was one of the few who did not reply).

In May I sent in a progress report to Burnett, asking to know his deadline and the arrangements for reimbursing me for postal and other expenses, as I was getting no honorarium. Burnett replied: "My business manager assures me that this good-neighbor gesture is not, at this moment feasible" and must be shelved "for some time". I wrote Burnett that the issue I was preparing "would have proved quite equal to *Story*'s standards", that his "good-neighbor" characterization carried more than a *soupçon* of patronage in it, and that I would not be available again until the war ended; would he now relieve me of some of the labour and embarrassment of apologizing to fifty authors? Burnett's reply, putting the responsibility on Smith for "jumping the gun", ended my correspondence with *Story*. When I broke the news to Hugh MacLennan (who was half-way through writing his story), he wrote me he was relieved, because Burnett had recently returned a novel to him which he had held for three months, sent back requiring revisions, kept the revised manuscript another nine months, and then rejected it without adequate comment. I presume this was *Two Solitudes*.

I was learning the hard way that commitments made to authors even by prestigious editors, especially by American ones dealing with Canadians, needed contractual backing before they were worth an hour of a writer's time. I was to be a slow learner. Fortunately, the stories I had already accepted I was able to pass on to Ralph Gustafson for an anthology of Canadian writing he was preparing (later published as *Canadian Accent*).

In those first months of 1942 I became aware that two young British poets were now living in Canada. From Montréal I was sent a copy of *Preview*, a mimeographed magazine with much cumbersome prose but some very lively and "contemporary" verse by Patrick Anderson, a newly arrived Englishman, and by Frank Scott. Then from a Dr. J. Wreford Watson, professor of geography at McMaster University in Hamilton, I received my first invitation to give a poetry reading. Watson and his wife Jessie, both recently from Scotland, had organized a faculty literary club at McMaster's (after being rebuffed by the local Canadian Authors' branch), and they wanted me to read my "David", which they had seen in the *Forum*, to their members. When I met the professor I discovered he had been writing and publishing poetry in Britain under the name of "James Wreford". He was embarrassed to disclose to his scientific colleagues at McMaster that he wrote poetry, and had been a member of an Edinburgh group which included such distinguished writers as Edwin Muir, David Daiches, and "Hugh McDiarmid". His own work, however, seemed to me much more influenced by Eliot and the Auden/Day-Lewis/Spender group.

After my Hamilton reading, Wreford and I began a lengthy, and for me most stimulating correspondence, which continued for some time. His detailed and appreciative reactions to my work heartened me to go on trying to market my *David* book; in turn I put him in touch with Patrick Anderson and other editors and anthologists. He became a contributor to *Preview*, was one of the *Unit of Five* writers in 1944, published two books and won the Governor-General's medal in 1950. Prof. Watson, however, was an even better scientist and soon after returned to his native city as Edinburgh University's Professor of Geography. He had remained there, publishing no more verse. When I visited him in the Seventies, I discovered that his teen-age children did not know he had ever written poetry. In 1979, however, he re-visited Canada, published a new chapbook, *Countryside Canada*, and is now a writer-in-residence at a Canadian university.

In '42, despite the war, the cause of "contemporary" poetry was on the upsurge in Canada. With important anthologies underway by Smith and Gustafson, the appearance of *Preview* in Montreal and a new magazine projected in the west which would involve Livesay and myself, the maple-leafers in the Canadian Authors' Association were on the defensive, even in Toronto. In April I wrote Gustafson that "the stage is almost set here for a new literary scene" and I instanced the launching of a *Canadian Review of Music and Art* by the Toronto Arts & Letters Club, and a recent talk I'd had with Ned Pratt. He was the only major writer in the country still giving allegiance to the Canadian Authors' Association; indeed he was titular editor of their "house organ", the *Canadian Poetry Magazine*; but, as he told me privately, in good round Newfie language, he was so fed up with the old farts moaning when he wouldn't print their crap that he was determined to resign and propose that the magazine either pack it up or get a younger editor of the calibre of Gustafson or myself. It seemed to me that, whatever happened to CPM , Canada was heading into a literary revival even in the middle of a war.

But now I was too involved in the war itself to share in this new scene. In May, before I had finished marking final exam papers, I was accepted for a rapid-training course in Personnel Selection and sworn into the Canadian Active Army. By the end of June I had taken indefinite leave from the university, qualified as an infantry officer at Brockville and been listed for overseas duty. Although it was another ten months before I actually sailed for Europe, I was from now on fully employed by the army in Ontario. I had to decline various invitations to write or submit poetry that were at last beginning to come my way, now that the *David* book was out and being favourably reviewed.

As much as possible, however, I kept up correspondence with old literary friends in the east, and in Vancouver with the McConnells and the Crawleys. I was able to help Livesay get her new book accepted by Ryerson, which had already taken A.J.M. Smith's. Even my sonneteer acquaintance from the Thirties, Robert Finch, was impressed enough with the critical acceptance of *David* (which went into two editions by February, '43) that he was putting together a book too. (It was not published, however, until 1944.) And I was happy to see the *Forum* still publishing a backlog of material I had left them, by Miriam Waddington, Klein and others, and bringing out Pratt's very fine *Truant*.

I was disappointed, however, with *Preview*, which was developing much pseudo-surrealist posing and calculated mystifying, becoming just an outlet for a small inverted group. Its new rival, *First Statement*, seemed to have more cash but little judgement, and though Crawley's *Contemporary Verse* was fulfilling its promise, its editor was not in a position to expand its size or improve its format. When I left Canada in May '43, the muse of poetry seemed still a starveling with few to admire her at home and none abroad.

I was busy with officer-selection duties at an encampment in England in September when a sergeant-majorish sort of letter reached me from Watson Kirkconnell, President of the Canadian Authors' Association, that I had "won the Sterling Silver Medal of the Governor General for Poetry". I was requested to prepare a fifteen-minute reply to the "presentation address" to be given (at a date already past) in the Royal York Hotel, Toronto. My wife, who had accepted the gong in my stead, now wrote me that the address was leaden and the medal not sterling. The same mail brought me a letter from Wreford telling me that Hamilton's biggest bookstore stocked no *David*s and recommended Robert Service instead. It was the same old Maple Leaf land.

During the next two years I had little correspondence with the Canadian *literati* — with the exception of the Crawley group and a surprising and generous fan letter from Sir Charles G.D. Roberts. Though my army work involved me in personally interviewing several thousand Canadian soldiers, none of them turned out to be writers, and apart from brief friendly moments with Mavor Moore at London headquarters, the only author from Canada I saw during my two years in Europe was Sinclair Ross. I discovered his unit was near mine briefly and managed to reach him by phone and persuade him to have a Sunday walk with me in a park. Ross, however, seemed quite overcome with my being in the major's uniform I was required to wear, and though he was on leave and in "civvies" he refused to stop calling me "sir", and remained monosyllabic till we parted. I still think he is a good fiction writer.

Through Cyril Connolly at *Horizon* and John Lehmann at *New Writing* I met a number of young English poets during weekend leaves in London, and I began to be published for the first time in England. In these circles there was almost total ignorance of even bad Canadian literature. Fortunately, Art Smith had sent me a copy of his first (1943) edition of the *Book of Canadian Poetry*. I passed it, and Gustafson's Penguin anthology around, and was encouraged with the interest they aroused. Soon I was asked to submit a talk on the "New Canadian Poetry" for the BBC. However, the producer couldn't get it scheduled unless I broadened the topic to include the whole range of CanLit (in 28 minutes). By the time I had that potted, and mentioned the only five writers the BBC authority had heard of (Service, Drummond, Pickthall, MacRae, and de la Roche) and squeezed in quotes from Lampman, Pratt, Livesay and Gustafson, and plugged MacLennan and Callaghan — my producer had been called up for army service. The talk was barely rescued from the scrap basket by a shortwave editor desperate for material. Eventually (July 1944) it was sandwiched into a program "The BBC Calling the West Indies" and probably listened to only by whatever bored Canadian soldiery were still stationed in Jamaica.

Still, it was a "first", of sorts. And the job had compelled me to read some authors in Smith's anthology whom I had previously avoided. I decided that anybody with an historical conscience was licked from the start; nineteenth century Canadiana was an overstuffed drawingroom of love-seats and embroidered snow-drops. A.J.M., it seemed to me, should put more time into his own poetry, which was becoming first-class (despite the fact that it too had now been given a G.G.) and less on Hevysege.

In September '44, while waiting in Sussex for a posting to the Continent, I got a circular from Montreal dated two months back with the signatures of Dudek, Klein and Patrick Anderson and two others unknown to me, Neuville Shaw and Irving Layton. It had not been addressed to me but to one of my *Forum* protegés out in Vancouver, Bill McConnell. It announced that these "available writers" had met to consider forming a "Dominion-wide organization" of "new and meaningful writers" in opposition to the CAA. They hoped to include Frank Scott, A.J.M. Smith, John Sutherland and somebody named Bruce Ruddick. As I wrote to Dorothy Livesay, I was not impressed with the representativeness of this list, which seemed to be made up simply of Montrealers, scarcely in a position to reform, let alone overthrow, the CAA.

I was taken, however, by the validity of their main program, which was to secure governmental grants for writers, CBC time for readings and reviews of Canadian writing, more modern literature in educational curricula, writers-in-residence in universities, a basic contract for authors, a national literary agency, and improved copyright protection. In effect, the Montreal group had outlined the literary causes for which I intended to campaign if I were spared to return to Canada.

During the last and coldest winter of the war I shuttled in a jeep over frozen flatlands along the Dutch-Belgian border, as the officer in charge of personnel re-allocations for the Canadian troops in Montgomery's army. There followed various sojourns in hospitals until, in May 1945, I was invalided back to the land of Hevysege, made to convalesce in Pauline Johnson's Vancouver, and discharged into the CAA's Toronto.

I was too restless, however, to slide easily into the niche being held for me in University College's cloister. By October I had moved myself and family to Montreal, where I had been offered (on the recommendation of Mavor Moore) a job supervising foreign language broadcasts for CBC's international shortwave service.

It was a challenging and responsible post which often kept me in the CBC for eleven hours at a stretch. I was still walking on two canes and, because of Ottawa's restriction on autos, using streetcars. On weekends, however, I gradually came to know personally most of the writers of Anglophone Montréal. Thirty-five years later I still count some of them as friends: Frank and Marion Scott, Louis Dudek, Hugh MacLennan, Irving Layton. Some were also colleagues, such as Mavor himself, and Eric Koch, René Garneau, Robert and Rita Allen. Others are still-loved ghosts: Abraham Klein, who took time more than once from an over-busy schedule to have lunch with me; Charles Wasserman, one of our "free-lancers"; and my colleague, Arthur Phelps. At one or two crowded parties I met Robert Choquette and, briefly, some of the younger Québec-English writers, including *Preview* and *First Statement* editors (notably Patrick Anderson and the late John Sutherland).

Although I was impressed with these groups I was depressed by their strident quarreling with each other and with their public, and I thought their aims still parochial and confused. I could see little hope in such groups challenging the organizational monopoly of the Canadian Authors' Association. Consequently, when Roy Daniells (by now the Head of English at the University of Manitoba) wrote asking me to contribute an article for a student review he was editing, I sent him the following diatribe on what I thought was wrong not so much with Canadian poetry as with English-Canadian poets.

1946

Has Poetry a Future in Canada?
Winnipeg, *Manitoba Arts Review*, Spring 1946.

Nobody knows the answer and not many people at present care. At least the question may provoke further questions — can poetry become a significant art form in this nation? — is the making of poetry an activity of consequence in Canada today?

Despite a good deal of optimistic talk about a "renaissance" in Canadian poetry at present, I think the answer to the last query is "No". It's difficult to generalize about anything in a country as heterogeneous as a Woolworth store (and one example of the difficulty is that my own ignorance limits me to the field of Canadian poetry in the English language) but I think a look at the facts will suggest that poetry is the least influential of the arts in Canada.

To begin with, there still does not breathe in this land a magazine of poetry with a quality or following anything like that achieved by *Canadian Art*, which publicizes painting and the other visual arts. There are, to my knowledge, three journals exclusively devoted to verse in Canada, each rather emaciated and appearing quarterly or fitfully to a few hundred readers at most. Only one of them, *Contemporary Verse*, has maintained, during three precarious years of mimeographed existence, a standard high enough to induce a responsible person to mention it to any stranger seriously interested in poetry. And how many of my readers (including, if I am not presuming, professors of English) have yet to read a copy of *Contemporary Verse*?

The University quarterlies, whose circulation is not much better, either refuse to publish verse at all (e.g. the *University of Toronto Quarterly*) or limit its appearance to about four per cent of their textual space. Most of what's printed is routinely "traditional", i.e., showing influences no more disturbing than those of the Georgian and Imagist schools of thirty years ago. The weekly *Saturday Night* allots about one per cent (about half the space for its cooking recipes) to serious verse, some of which is readable and the rest appears to have been chosen as a kind of decorative cement to fill gaps left by articles which failed to reach the bottom of a column. The *Canadian Forum*, though discussing poetry with its usual high seriousness, is not above the same impromptu plasterer's approach to the problem of publication. It pays nothing, prints the best that wanders in, and hopes for better. That it sometimes prints the best in Canada is not a vindication of its policy but a further proof that good verse, particularly if it contains ideas unfriendly to the *status quo,* is lucky to receive the benefit of type at all in this land of maple leaves and pulpwood millionaires.

And what of the organs of mass circulation, the daily press, the Sunday supplements, the slick national monthlies? Despite their affluence and longevity, I do not believe that any one of them has yet published a single example of the better poetry written in this country. A recent poem by E.J. Pratt in *Maclean's* is a not so notable exception: *Maclean's* waited twenty years before accepting E.J. Pratt and then published one of his weaker poems, after excising its strongest stanza. The amount of rhythmic utterance hidden within the voluminous folds of a Canadian daily ranges from nothing to one-tenth of one per cent; of this, most are the trashiest sort of rhyming and the rest are generally pirated extracts from current anthologies.

The present year has seen the birth of two new Canadian magazines (*Reading* and *Northern Review*) with a poetry content of eight and twenty per cent respectively, each interested in poetry as an art form and each willing to pay for it. In a year's time it will be easier to tell whether these two are portents of a new age or the newest victims of an old.* So far no Canadian monthly has been able to survive by devoting itself mainly to creative literature, whether prose or poetry.

What of publication outside the country? The names of Canadian poets who appear in American or British magazines of quality can be counted on the fingers, and the appearance of a book of Canadian verse from a reputable foreign publishing house is as rare as a twenty-one gun salute.

At first glance, the annual bibliographies of poetry published in Canada might suggest a happier situation in regard to book publications. In 1942 the *University of Toronto Quarterly* listed about thirty-five new volumes of verse by Canadians. A second glance shows, however, that about half of these were tiny chapbooks printed at the author's expense, limited to two or three hundred copies, and circulating only at further cost to their begetters. Four years later, it is possible to say that only three of the thirty-five went into a second edition (i.e. sold more than 500 copies) and none is now in print. It is true that some of the best-known Canadian poets did not publish during that year; but it is also true that some of those whose names appear in every honour roll of contemporary poets have yet to see any one of their books sell five hundred copies.

The Canadian poet most celebrated and most read today — and

Reading was defunct in a year; *Northern Review* died with its founder, John Sutherland, in 1956.

deservedly — is E.J. Pratt; yet not one of his volumes has sold as widely as any of a score of cheap, highly touted and already forgotten "Canadian Novels" appearing in the last ten years.

This is a state of affairs which is now assumed by Canadian publishers to be normal. A book of poetry is expected to be by its nature unpalatable to the average Canadian reader, and therefore advertising expense is kept to the minimum sufficient to ensure a certain "prestige" for the publishing house in case the poet becomes famous in spite of all. Even if that happens, little added effort will be made to advertise him or to make use of the hundred and one promotional devices which any publisher employs to peddle the wares of even the cheapest and most ephemeral novelist. The publisher, of course, has invested more of his precious paper allotment in a novel, and more advertising money; also, there is always a possibility that a novel might become a best-seller. The poet is permitted, at the most, a *succès d'estime.*

With such an attitude on the part of publishers — and a scrutiny of their advertisements in any newspaper will prove the point — it is not surprising that for book reviewers, too, poetry is the Cinderella of our arts. The literary editors of most newspapers either ignore it entirely or confine themselves to a belated rehash of the biography on the dustcover. And the review will normally take second place on the bookpage to that of any sentimental romance which happens to be the momentary focus of promotion by a foreign publishing house. Our literary journals make some effort to discuss the poetry itself but in most of them the quality of the reviewing is so wretched that neither the author nor his book is helped. The typical Canadian reviewer of poetry has no knowledge of contemporary techniques or contemporary poets abroad; he is inclined to consume precious space denouncing lapses from Presbyterian morality or mid-Victorian diction, to be top-lofty about any experimentation, and to condemn as bad any poem which would not be immediately intelligible to a ten-year-old. There are exceptions, of course, but few among the reviewers in organs of wide circulation.

No doubt some of these statements are true for all the arts in Canada, but they are not true to the same extent. There is scarcely a town over fifty thousand population in Canada which does not have an art gallery with at least a few Canadian paintings of contemporary vintage on display. In the larger cities, fixed or travelling exhibits of modern painters are now frequent, and Canadian art circulates more and more widely by means of picture-loan societies. Canadian composers of music have been notoriously neglected — yet scarcely a week goes by without a radio presentation of the work of some native composer, not to speak of the growing tendency to include Canadian work in the programs of string quartets and soloists in various cities. Our painting has been exhibited successfully both in England and America, and our handicrafts are a steady marketable commodity both inside and outside our boundaries. Yet, with the exception of the small paperback anthology of Canadian verse edited by Ralph Gustafson (and it is a gratifying exception), our poetry is virtually unknown to the peoples in the United Kingdom or the other members of the British Commonwealth.

What are the reasons for all this? Without a doubt they are not simple. Professor E.K. Brown, in his very important book *On Canadian Poetry*, reminds us that our population is only twelve million, of whom one-third are French-speaking, and that in consequence a Canadian author — especially since he is in competition with Americans — has not enough customers to earn a living in his own country. He reminded us also that we are still somewhat puritan in expressed sentiments — an attitude hostile to good poetry — and still not free of that "colonial complex" which regards its own cultural products as necessarily second-rate. Later, in a stirring radio talk on "The Neglect of Canadian Literature",* Professor Brown attacked the sheer lack of *interest* by Canadians in their own writers, as the thing most in the way of a development of our culture.

Much as I agree with Professor Brown's analysis, I do not feel it supplies the whole answer. In respect to his first point, it can be said that although we Canadians are not legion, we are three times as numerous as the people of Ireland in the days when books by Yeats and other Irishmen were read and borrowed and sold in tens of thousands in their own land and by hundreds of thousands abroad. There are few countries so small in Europe or elsewhere that have not at one time or another produced an important poet. It is true also that most great poets, including Shakespeare, had to find a living by other means than selling their poetry — yet it did not prevent them from becoming great poets. There are a number of persons of very limited literary talent who make a steady living in this country by journalism or radio script-writing; are these fields barred to the better writer? I do not think so. If economic independence were necessary to the writing of twentieth century poetry, we should not have heard of E.A. Robinson, Robert Frost, Carl Sandburg, Vachel Lindsay or T.S. Eliot. The idea that poetry must wait for a leisured or professionally poetic class is a nineteenth century British delusion; in the face of a roster of the best poets of America or of twentieth century Britain, it fails to explain anything.

It is true, of course, that our national newness and rawness are not conducive to poetry. Our ancient rich and our *nouveaux riches* find the making of another million more satisfying than being known as patrons of letters. There are no scholarships for poets, no glittering thousand-dollar competitions from publishers, no Yadda, and no

* First published in *Civil Service Review XVII* (1944) 307-9.

72

endowments for chairs of creative writing in our universities. In all these matters we are singularly out of step with modern American life. The typical Canadian classifies a poet among the "long-hairs", and is surprised if he meets one and finds him normally dressed and shaven. We have no bookstores like the best in London or New York, where it is a point of honour to give poetry an equal display with any other branch of letters, and for the salesclerk to know something about the contents of what he is selling.

Yet when all this has been said, when we have properly berated the publishers and booksellers, the editors and journalists, the reviewers and professors, the selfish rich and the indifferent poor — have we really covered the ground? Is it not possible that our poets themselves may be partly to blame for the lowly status of their art?

I am not here concerned with the inevitable jingle-ladies of both sexes who are present in all countries at all times, the people who write rhymed lines in the same spirit as schoolboys sell hotdogs at ball games, for pin money, or as schoolgirls make scrapbooks of movie heroes, to project their uniformed passions. It is unfortunate that sometimes they band themselves into societies which pretend to speak for Canada in the name of poetry, but again it is less their fault than the real poets', if their wares are taken for the best. Our Canadian painters have not found it necessary to complain that they are confused in the public mind with the itinerants who produce "genuine original" water colours of jade mountains and maroon lakes at a half-hour's notice. No, it is the serious artist in words who should take stock of himself in Canada today.

We complain that there is no adequate magazine for poetry in this country. Are the poets wholly blameless for this situation when they have persistently banded themselves into camps, each preferring to damn the other through the medium of its mimeographed "house-organ" rather than pool talents and money for the production of one good and financially stable journal? "Schools" and cliques beget poetasting; the great poets were not members of coteries.

We complain that reviewers are stupid — yet how seldom do we behold a poet defending himself in print or arguing with a reviewer? The foolish critic who is challenged in his follies will either avoid reviewing your next book or review it with more caution; in either case, you can't lose.

We complain that the established magazines and newspapers pay little or nothing for our work and take little or nothing of it. Yet if, to feed the vanity of being in print, we are willing to undercut each other's price, our artist's fee, even to the point of giving our work away, can we expect that commercially-minded editors will place any monetary value on our products? If the twenty best writers of verse in this country got together and set a reasonable minimum rate (say, three cents a word) for their work, the better journals would pay it, and they would have more respect for poets. The demand for the work of a good painter normally increases with the price he sets on his canvases....

How many poets ever try to advertise themselves? A good Canadian painter does not feel he has lowered himself in the eyes of his fellow-artists when he puts on a one-man show, or gives an interview to the press about his work and his plans. How many Canadian poets today ever give a public — or, for that matter, a private — reading of their work? Ned Pratt is an exception, and a significant one, of which more later. In some cases, where the poet has not learned how to read aloud, it is just as well — yet what a pitifully meagre concept of a poet's art that he should write only for the printed page and be incapable of "playing" his own carefully-wrought rhythms and word-patterns with the instrument of his own voice. I have talked to earnest *avant-garde* poets in Canada who appear to believe that only a charlatan would give a reading of his own poetry. Some of them do not even seem to be aware that, from the beginnings of man's history, the art of poetry has been an art of oration as well as of transcription. Poetry is composed for the ear; it is written down in order to be preserved; but it can only be fully enjoyed and transmitted by the blessed sound of the human voice. Canadian poets need to go out barn-storming again, as Carman and Roberts were not ashamed to do, as C. Day Lewis and other outstanding English poets do today, as Whitman and Lindsay and Frost and Sandburg and a host of others have done, and some still do, even in the America we are fond of picturing as more Philistine than ourselves.

If our younger poets could be persuaded and helped to hire a hall (or a radio program), put out handbills, and challenge the interest of their potential public, I think they would discover many things of profit to themselves and to the future of Canadian letters. They would find, as Professor Pratt has found, that the people of this country will turn out to hear poetry read, and turn out in hundreds in the larger cities, and come again in larger numbers. They would discover, too, that they themselves would get to be known and influential as *poets*, instead of as professors, or newspapermen, or whatever else. Also, they would begin the necessary education of the Canadian public to the fact that good poets are not freaks, that, as Eric Gill said, "the artist is not a special kind of man, but every man is a special kind of artist."

Finally, they will learn that the reading of poetry under such circumstances supplies a rather shrewd test of the social value of their own art — that the pleasure of writing something so equivocally and capriciously that no one else can really know what you mean, is a pleasure that evaporates if you stand up before the eyes and ears of people who have given up an evening to be emotionally affected by your

74

words. For the delights of the coterie and the ephemeral private joke would be substituted the satisfaction and achievement of saying something which, though moulded out of your own personality and imagination and feeling, was nevertheless so moulded as to convey in its very sounds and surges the mysteries of thought and passion common to all men. To see that happen before one's eyes, to create a synthesis for others out of your own conflicts, is surely a sufficient reward and a stimulus to correct the tortuous shallowness of so much fashionable verse-writing in Canada today.

For the truth is that one of the things most wrong about recent Canadian poetry is the deliberate unintelligibility of some of our most gifted poets. Part of it is a juvenile bravado, a sort of father-revolt. Since Roberts and his school wrote simply, the new generation scorns to be easily understood, just as they are contemptuous of "nature" or anything "pleasant", of narrative or ballad or straight lyric. They walk in fear of being uncerebral, sentimental, or popular. They are inclined to specialize, therefore, in the tortuous cryptic satire and pseudo-philosophical charade — in poetry, that is, which they cannot read aloud even to their own followers.

It is dangerous for a poet to be contemptuous of his public, or to salve himself with the romantic hope that because he is not understood today he will be all the greater tomorrow. The atomic age is no time to be indulging in verbal exhibitionism and the expectation of literary immortality. The human race does not look indestructible any longer and a poet might just as well reconcile himself to his present audience. Certainly, no audience in the future is more likely to need poetic idealism than the present one. Obscurantism is also a sign of intellectual snobbery, of an assumption that the ordinary man is not worth writing to. Yet there is a large proportion of our population who listen to good music, and respond to it more markedly the better it is played; these ears are ready for good poetry too, if the words carry clearly the message of a meaning.

The most pointless plaint for a poet to make (though it is well that the critic makes it) is that Canada is not "mature" enough for his poetry. Until the poet acquires enough self-confidence in this country to realize that he is part of what makes it mature, there will be no maturation and no great poetry. A poet, living or dead, is of significance in his own country when his lines come naturally to the mind of succeeding writers, when they are naturally quoted by our preachers, radio speakers and professors, and spontaneously misquoted by our statesmen. There will always be a time-lag, of course, but one of the reasons that even our most literate public figures continue to prefer quotations from Tennyson or Whitman or Milton is that no modern Canadian poet has said anything as pertinent for our generation and country as these poets said for their own.

There is a great desire on the part of many of our best younger poets to say important things *about* the world today, true — but there is little desire to say it *to* the world, and less even to say it to their own countrymen. It is fashionable among the "Montreal Group" and other Canadian poetry cliques today to talk about the need for "cosmopolitanism"; in fact, poets are praised or damned according as they appear to write "international" or "national" poetry.... Internationalism, however, often turns out to be only belated imitation of the technique of surrealism, certainly a cult conceived in Europe, but by poets more concerned with literary exhibitionism than with reaching the masses with their allegedly revolutionary ideas. The Roberts school of poetry is rightly criticized nowadays for its over-dependence on the poetry of nineteenth century England and America, yet some of our most talented young poets today who are the most forthright in such criticism are betraying still another "colonial" time-lag in their dependence on the poetic credos and techniques of writers abroad. Dylan Thomas and Kenneth Fearing and Aragon replace Keats and Whitman and Hugo. One looks almost in vain for serious attempts to find a technique, an attitude, above all a vocabulary and rhythm natural and native to Canada.

Cosmopolitanism, furthermore, is confused with an urban snobbery in respect to the value of rural and regional themes — and most of all by the poets who know only a fragment of Canada itself. A poet who writes about the beauty of prairie wheat is automatically rated below one who writes about the ugliness of city streets. The latter topic of course has more social significance — except to the farmer. A revolutionary approach to the world today is somehow associated with a revolt against syntax and the beauties of lucidity. In all this what is lost sight of is that the true cosmopolite in poetry, the great world figure, always had his roots deep in the peculiar soil of his own country, and made himself international because he spoke from his own nation even when he spoke for and to the world. There is room for the view that national boundaries are now politically regrettable; but they are a reality no poet should avoid; and when they cease to exist, there will long remain boundaries, however shadowy, of speech and culture and climate; and what a dull world otherwise, especially for the poet. An international attitude does not in itself make a poet one whit better as a poet· if the loyalty is to a mechanistic rather than a humanistic international·nalism, it may quite stultify his creative genius.

Meantime the most cosmopolitan service a Canadian poet can do is to make himself such a clear and memorable and passionate interpreter of Canadians themselves, in the language of Canada, that the world will accept him as a mature voice, and be the readier for that to accept Canada as a mature nation. Canada has still an opportunity to contribute greatly to the healing of this desperately sick but curable world.

She cannot, for all the talk of "middle-powers", play a decisive role physically, but she can and will be accepted as a world force when she produces thinkers and statesmen and artists of world calibre. And the poets of Canada will qualify, and answer positively the question with which I began, when and if they realize that their audience is not the outmoded pseudo-Bohemian flat on a Saturday night, or the antediluvian Poetry Séance, but the great mass of men and women in this country (who constitute also the most neglected subject matter for Canadian poetry). Then they will write not like expatriate dilettantes, or backwoodsmen either, but like men who are the flowering of a hundred nations, who have a unique and fateful role to play in this desperate world, . . . and have eyes equally alert to the pages of *Pravda* and the exact shade of fuzz on a prairie poplar leaf.

As I Remember

1946: January - September

At the beginning of 1946 I was still totally involved in my CBC job, and coming to realize that my spirits as well as my physical health were suffering from both the long hours and the rigours of the Montreal climate. Consequently, after turning down academic offers in climates even worse, I was ready to listen when President Norman ("Larry") MacKenzie approached me one March day on an Ottawa train and offered to match whatever was my present salary with a post as professor of Anglosaxon and medieval English literature at my old alma mater, UBC. After reassurances that I would be free of Summer School duties, and could institute a yearly credit workshop in creative writing, I accepted and gave CBC due notice of resignation as of mid-June.

Meanwhile I heard from the Governor-General's Awards Committee that my *Now is Time* had won me a second poetry medal; it would be presented to me in Toronto at a July convention of the Canadian Authors' Association. On the heels of this notice came a letter from William Arthur Deacon, the Toronto Globe & Mail's literary editor, writing as president of the CAA and offering me the editorship of the *Canadian Poetry Magazine*. The offer was couched more in the way of a demand. Watson Kirkconnell, who had taken over as editor when Pratt resigned, was dropping out too. (He had recently published in CPM a hostile review of *Now is Time*.) I was the logical choice, wrote Deacon, for a three-year term. I must accept, if only as a favour to "the organization which has twice honoured you". I had not realized till then that he was also the Chairman of the G.G. Awards and I was startled at Deacon's assumption the CAA and a Governor-General's Committee were all the same people.

I felt no personal obligation to either; but I realized that this might be the chance to transform what was now only a feeble house-organ of Old Guard poetasters into that national outlet for contemporary work and criticism that every good young poet in Canada wanted. Before deciding I got Larry MacKenzie's assurance he would welcome the magazine to the UBC campus, and Ned Pratt's warm promise of support. Coming to Toronto in June I got Deacon's consent to the transfer of the magazine's office to Vancouver and promise of complete editorial independence for me, and my control of the other editorial appointments.

Deacon also agreed, somewhat reluctantly, to my proposal to explore with Alan Crawley the possibility of a collaboration between his *Contemporary Verse* and the new CPM. Crawley, the previous winter, despite his lack of sight had made a most successful tour with his wife Jean through Canada, reciting poems from earlier issues of his magazine and meeting the leading younger poets who were his main contributors. I wanted in no way to be put in a position of competition with him; yet I knew both Alan and Jean were determined not to expand the size of their tiny multigraphed quarterly, and had more than enough physical and financial difficulties maintaining even that. I hoped we might arrive at some sort of joint editorial and financing arrangement which would preserve the identity and solvency of both periodicals as partners in the building of a quarterly with the prestige of Chicago *Poetry* but essentially Canadian.

To some extent I knew what Deacon was getting me into. He was an able journalist, an energetic editor, and a good judge of popular taste; his review could launch or sink a new Canadian book. But poetry, except for the sort exhibited in his *Four Jameses*, was not his bailiwick. CPM was important to him only as a vehicle bringing prestige and members to his CAA (which I and my associate editors now would be required to join). It was doing neither, since Pratt left, and he wanted me to do both. What troubled me was that I would have no control over the business of the magazine, which would remain for the present in the hands of a retired Toronto lawyer named A.H. O'Brien who was holed up in his Muskoka home for the summer and not even available for meeting before I had to take off for Vancouver.

My fears were soon sharpened when, established in a temporary office on the UBC campus, I got my first letter from O'Brien. It was to tell me he had decided to continue having the magazine printed in Toronto, and to retain most of the present associate editors, adding Audrey Alexander Brown and perhaps other well-known CAA members to the Board. His letter concluded by exhorting me not to "swing too much to the left" but keep to "the middle of the road". I of course replied at once that I would make my own decisions, based on craftsmanship and originality, two virtues which I found lacking in recent issues of the journal. I said I was choosing all the editors myself, with an eye to regional representation and poetic achievement. I said what I needed from him was letterhead stationery, money for postage and typing services from the fund Deacon had told me the Business Manager had been given for these purposes, a back file of recent issues, and information as to the number of pages of text I would need to supply for the September issue after he had calculated the space required for Kirkconnell's holdover and for advertising. I also wanted to know who would make up the final dummy and read the page proofs.

By mid-August I had heard nothing from O'Brien. Instead the mail brought me from Kirkconnell a wad of previously accepted material, most of it of such abysmal quality even Kirkconnell labelled it "feeble". I reduced the pile to six poems, and stepped up my own search for more and better stuff. Esther, my wife, pitched in to help me with the now quickly mounting correspondence, as I continued to send out feelers to prospective sub-editors and contributors. Response, though slow, was encouraging: from the Ottawa-Montreal area, promises of poems from Page and Klein, and agreements to serve as regional editors from Pat Waddington and (for the prairies) Anne Marriott. From Charles Bruce in the Maritimes I got a promise to look for east coast poems, though he declared himself personally fed-up both with Deacon's CAA-empire building and E.K. Brown's academic Brahminism, and was marketing his own work now in the States. I was beginning to feel some sympathy with his viewpoint.

It was as well I had started early looking for new copy. In August I heard again from Kirkconnell, asking me to airmail 30 typed pages of poetry at once to O'Brien's office, care of a Mrs. Cannon, who it seems was his secretary. The next day came a great package of books to be reviewed. The Birneys were now in the middle of buying furniture and moving it into a shack without a telephone in the emergency housing area for professors near the UBC campus. I bethought myself that the Vancouver branch of the CAA had written welcoming me to membership and saying how wonderful it was that CPM was now being edited from Vancouver. They were having a meeting that week and I went to it and made an appeal for volunteer typists and reviewers. Nobody volunteered.

Somehow Esther found time for the typing, and I wrote and mailed off the reviews in the last week of August at the Elphinstone summer institute in between lecturing on modern literature. When I came back to the campus on the first of September I found a letter from O'Brien, posted from his summer hideout, to tell me he "would like the September CPM to come out on time" and would "therefore" list Kirkconnell as its editor. He added that there were no back issues available to me, nor stationery, and no money to pay contributors without the consent of the CAA's national executive, of which he was a member. It was now plain to me I was dealing with a man both incompetent and, for unknown reasons, hostile. I wrote him there would be no September issue unless the promises of Deacon and Pratt to begin paying contributors were honoured — and my name included in the masthead as at least joint editor.

While waiting to hear from the mysterious East I arranged a meeting with Crawley and his west-coast editors. I was too alarmed about O'Brien now to raise the possibility of amalgamation with CV but we agreed to exchange mailing lists and information about possible contributors; our journals remained on the friendliest terms during the remainder of my editorship.

It was another ten days before the galley proofs arrived. In the Forties airmail required extra postage — and O'Brien had sent the galleys at surface rates. By working through the night I got them back into the post the next morning. The day after came a letter from O'Brien complaining I hadn't returned the proofs! In the same letter he told me the National Executive had now agreed to paying contributors, but it would be ten cents a line not fifteen. Fortunately on the same date as his letter, Pratt had meantime phoned me that the fifteen cents rate was confirmed, and warned me that O'Brien was nearly eighty years old and "a mite fuzzy now".

The September issue finally appeared in October. It was full of proof errors as a result of emendations to my copy made by O'Brien for reasons he never explained. The make-up was a ragbag.

The New *Canadian Poetry Magazine*

Editorial, September 1946.

With this number, the *Canadian Poetry Magazine* changes editors and, to some extent, policy. The system of awarding prizes for the best three poems, and granting honourable mention to three others, is suspended. Instead, all poetry published will be paid for at a uniform rate. This change will bring our magazine in line with the *Dalhousie Review*, *Queen's Quarterly*, *Saturday Night* and other Canadian journals paying for verse, and enable us to compete with them on equal terms. Moreover, it will establish ours as the only Canadian journal devoted to poetry and paying for what it prints. It is now the poets of this country who are challenged; we are providing them with a professional medium for their work; it is up to them to make this magazine not only the best in Canada, but a magazine that will not suffer by comparison with the best in the United States and Great Britain. We believe there is sufficient poetry of good quality being written in this country to produce such a magazine; we appeal to the poets to make our belief an actuality.

... We do not wish, by such an appeal, to be understood as asking poets to sever their relations with other journals in order to offer loyalty to us. The amount of space available for periodical publication of verse in this country is pitifully small: there is room for all of us. It is true that the existence of many small poetry magazines tends to prevent any one journal from building up financial stability and a satisfactory circulation, and we are, therefore, at all times ready to discuss with other journals the possibility of amalgamation under our banner. We believe, however, that the *Canadian Poetry Magazine* has a name and a tradition to be restored and developed. It is by far the oldest magazine of poetry in Canada and the only one planned on a national scale and supported by a national body of writers....

We are at present forming an editorial board of men and women who are themselves writing poetry of distinction. They are being selected also with a view to regional representation, so that we may gain contact with new and old voices in every part of the country. We are happy to number among these the name of a former Editor-in-Chief, Dr. E.J. Pratt, our greatest living poet, and Charles Bruce, an outstanding Canadian journalist and a poet of ever widening reputation. Other names will be announced in our next issue.

In choosing the "best", your new Editor-in-Chief frankly intends to be eclectic. We are not out to serve any coterie or any narrow theory of poetry. We will insist always on two virtues, neither of which can stand alone: craftsmanship and originality. We do not value rhyming above assonance, the sonnet above free verse, or consider flawless metrics sufficient excuse to publish banalities. "Obscurity" in itself will not form a basis either for rejection or acceptance. There is just as much room for variety of technique in poetry as in painting or music, and we will not condemn a poem because, like much of Shakespeare, it needs several readings before the full meaning emerges, nor will we print a poem which seems to us to contain nothing but a deliberate and fashionable obscurity which darkens further under scrutiny. We believe that poetry is a means of communication between men, and, of all verbal means, the most memorable. We are not primarily concerned then with whether the poet is "left-wing" or "right-wing", "experimental" or "classical". We are concerned with the success of his attempt to express a genuine and understandable emotion through a form which re-creates a similar emotion in the reader. That is why we shall welcome contributions both from poets who have appeared in the *Northern Review* and *Contemporary Verse*, and from many who have been our own contributors in the past. . . .

Finally, a word about some of the contributors to this issue. We are proud to be the first journal to print the work of Dr. Roy Daniells, professor of English in the University of British Columbia, and, for the first time, four poems by the late Fl. Sgt. Bertram J. Warr, R.A.F. In his few years of adulthood, which ended when he was conscripted in England and shot down over Germany in 1942, Warr wrote poems that won him publication in English magazines of quality. Several of these poems have been republished recently in *Contemporary Verse*, and a memorial prize established in his name. The poems appearing in this issue have never been previously published and have been secured through the courtesy of Miss Mary Warr. . . . Patrick Waddington, a contributor of short stories and poems to *Northern Review* and other journals, is assistant news editor for the International Shortwave Service of the C.B.C. . . . Miriam Waddington, his wife, is a Montreal social worker and author of a recent book of verse, *Green World*. . . . Dorothy Livesay, author of two books of poetry, including the current *Day and Night*, winner of the Governor-General's Award for Poetry in 1944, is a Vancouver journalist who is leaving shortly for Europe, where she will act as a foreign correspondent for the Toronto *Daily Star*. . . .

As I Remember

1946: October - December

Despite everything, the reactions to the first of the new CPMs were encouraging, at least from people whose judgements I respected. Pratt, Anderson, Souster, the Waddingtons, Klein, Gustafson, Livesay, Dudek, Floris McLaren, all took the trouble to write me that the quality both of the poetry and the reviews had plainly improved. Submissions were now coming in from most of the fifty poets I had canvassed. Only Layton, of the *First Statement* group, Ruddick and Shaw of *Preview*, and of course the French-Canadians, were to ignore all my blandishments. In Vancouver the CAA branch came to life, inviting me to "give an address" on behalf of CPM. As a result they announced a "drive" for new and younger CAA members, and for subscriptions. Though little came of it except more rejected manuscripts, the mails were beginning to bring in subscriptions from friends and unsolicited manuscripts of interest. Thanks to Marcus Adeney, the editor-musician whose *Review of Music and Art* had published my "Vancouver Lights" back in 1941, I received some of the poems of Anne Wilkinson, whom I would not have had the courage to approach. And Anne Marriott, my associate editor, conjured a poem and warm messages from Duncan Campbell Scott.

The president of another cultural body, the Vancouver Arts & Letters Club, wrote: "we are delighted that so distinguished a poet should have been added to the English Department at UBC." Would I "give us a talk on some subject, perhaps not *too* technically!..." I replied at once I would come, without fee, any time to read them poems from the new CPM and from my own books, and say not a word about techniques. But they never replied. A downtown reporter phoned me for an interview in the mistaken belief I was editing a Canadian poultry magazine.

I was determined the December issue would be twice as good, but by October I was up to the eyes in university work which took precedence. I had now begun UBC's first seminar in "creative writing". The usual academic straightjacket had been applied, however, even before registration day. Though I had asked that enrollment be limited to twenty and that applications should be entertained from students in any undergraduate faculty, it was decreed that only fourth year students could apply. The twenty I selected (on the basis of submissions of prose or poetry) proved a lively and challenging group. Several were youthful veterans. One of them at least, Mario Prizek, went on to a creative career in CBC production.

84

An immediate practical question raised by the more academic of my writer-students was: what was to be "assigned reading" in such a course? I had distributed, at the first class, my own basic bibliographies of contemporary English-language literature, based on UBC library holdings. But the library's funds for current books were scanty, and some of my students could not afford to buy their own. They could afford, however, to subscribe to at least one Canadian magazine. We devoted a workshop to examining a dozen available journals; as a result I was able to forward several subscriptions to each of the *Forum, Northern Review, Contemporary Verse* and *Saturday Night*. With professorial cunning, which I still recall with shame, I explained to the class I had kept CPM off their list, lest I be accused of nepotism. The result was a dozen additional subscriptions.

I was myself increasingly interested in both radio and film as outlets for the young literary talents. In October I proposed to President MacKenzie that the university library begin assembling a record collection of Canadian literature and plan a complete recording room at UBC with first-rate equipment both fixed and movable. Among my objectives were the preservation of public reading performances by visiting poets (Ned Pratt and Vachel Lindsay had given successful readings here without leaving a sonic trace); the collecting of available recordings of British and American poets (such as the Harvard Vocarium series) and of play productions; and the procuring from the CBC of copies or discards from their disc archives of relevant programs. I believed such a scheme was crucial to the development of modern studies in music, drama and literature, as well as to the development of a university or student radio station.

Though Larry MacKenzie was always open to new ideas, the university was being flooded with post-war enrollments; more basic needs had first to be met. So he asked me to form a committee to include the Librarian, the Heads of English and Music, and Ira Dilworth, regional Head of the CBC. With Ira I worked out the costs; they approximated fifteen thousand for the first year and ten thousand for succeeding ones. It sounds so little today, but it was too much for the budgeters of UBC in 1946. The Librarian did his best to expand the pathetic holdings in modern poetry (twelve poets, Yeats and eleven elderly Americans, no Canadians) from his regular budget. Our committee was kept "on the books" for years, without power or money. Sometime in the Fifties a now well-heeled Extension Department set up its own Audio-Visual Aids to Education Committee (including none of us), which assembled complete equipment: discs, films, projectors, etc., for classroom studies. And the students developed their own radio station. I was glad to see it all happen even though, in the process, CanLit dropped from sight and hearing.

Meantime, in those last months of '46, if I had an idle moment there was always *CPM*. In a letter to Pat Waddington on November 9 I tell him that Esther has had to revive her highschool shorthand and that we have just counted fifty-one letters waiting to be answered. (I am determined that the December issue will come out in December.) I am dictating in the Camp while bulldozers rip out the forest that begins fifty yards away over a sea of mud, and our ramshackle hut trembles periodically from the dynamite blasts of a stumping crew. After supper I will nip out to drag alder trunks and roots to my backdoor sawhorse — food for the Winnipeg heater, our only source of warmth against Vancouver's raw November. Then I will settle down to marking my weekly batch of a hundred freshman and sophomore "themes". Tomorrow night I must read a score of short stories from the writers' workshop. The following night I give my weekly two-hour extension lecture. On the 22nd I am writing Waddington again to send names of potential subscribers, contributors, donors, in Montreal. What about Anne Hébert? I want *CPM* to publish the best good French-Canadian poets, and in their language. . . .

In December I made an analysis of *CPM*'s subscriber list. We had risen to five hundred: one in PEI, 190 in Ontario, B.C. second with 87. There were 52 in the U.S. I sent the list off to O'Brien along with copies of fifty letters received in praise of the new *CPM* — with copies to Deacon. I took the occasion to ask him why three of the five persons making up *CPM*'s Management Committee (Amabel King, Jacob Markowitz, Watson Kirkconnell) hadn't written me at all about the September issue, for or against. I was beginning to get rumours from the east that these three wanted to sack me, and I wanted things out in the open. O'Brien's reaction, however, was to ask me if I wanted a higher stipend than the fifty dollars per quarter I was getting for running the magazine. He reminded me that Kirkconnell had worked for nothing. I tried to answer him patiently — he *was* an old man — by reminding him that, before I took on the editorship, I had time to write articles and poems and broadcasts which paid me many times more, and that I was running the editorial office without paid supplies or assistance.

At least the December issue came out in December.

Three Important Young Poets: Page, Dudek, Anderson

review of *As Ten, As Twenty* by P.K. Page, *East of the City* by Louis Dudek, and *The White Centre* by Patrick Anderson; *Canadian Poetry Magazine*, December 1946.

Congratulations to the Ryerson Press. Within the space of a month, they have published, in pleasant format, the first full-scale volumes of verse by three of the most important younger poets in Canada. All three have been known for some years to readers of Canadian and American literary journals, and Page and Dudek were among the five poets under thirty years of age who were printed in Ronald Hambleton's anthology, *Unit of Five*, two years ago. . . .

That these three have stature, despite their youth, is undeniable. All three are thoroughly contemporary in form and in ideas; they have been influenced by Auden, Dylan Thomas, and by some American poets, . . . but each has digested the influences. Every one of their poems has the stamp of intelligence, sensitivity and craftsmanship. And what is more remarkable among Canadian poets, all three write without sentimentality and without clichés.

The limitations they share are likewise unusual among our poets, and therefore the easier to accept in patience. All three have a certain coldness of atmosphere (Anderson the least), a touch of intellectual standoffishness even at the moment of kinship with the common people; yet even this is an effect rather than an attitude, a by-product of strongmindedness, their repudiation of easy tearjerking and banal conformity. Their verse is marked, to quote a critic, by "an abundance of intellectual concentration" (at times a super-abundance) and by "a preference for word-patterns rather than poetry" and "for the unnatural exploitation of the vivid image."

Perhaps these are faults of which Dudek, at least, is unaware, for the phrases quoted are his (*Preview*, Aug., 1944) and he applied them not to his own poetic circle, but to eleven alleged professor-poets in Canada, in whom he considered these faults inevitable, economically determined by their "retreat into the ivy-wreathed tower." Now that Dudek, a McGill graduate, is reported to be in pursuit of his doctorate in English from Columbia University, he may well feel in danger of infection, but the truth is that these characteristics were evident in his own work far more than in Pratt's. . . . Perhaps all this proves is that good poets can be bad critics, especially when newly under the spell of theories of economic fatalism, and that intellectualism and imagic cleverness are general excesses of the poetry of our time.

In P.K. Page's poetry, the psychological element dominates. One is aware of a pertinacity and a deadliness in the probing of mind, her own and others, a clinical interest in the moods of children, the mental habits of adolescents, of prisoners, the physically or mentally sick, landladies, stenographers, business men *l'homme moyen sensuel*. She has an x-ray trick of penetrating beyond surfaces, either of substance or of manner, into the matrix of her theme. It is perhaps significant that "eyes" are a recurrent source of metaphor to the point of obsession. The psychological portrait is in itself, however, only the outward cloak, in many of her poems, for an allegorical portrait, for a human pattern pregnant with the moral and intellectual dilemmas of our time. There is a visible progress here from her poems in *Unit of Five* (not included in this selection), progress from an at times hypercritical assertion of separateness to a positive, though somewhat obscurely expressed, identification with others "moving as we would move and qualifying death. . . . As ten, as twenty, now, we break from single thought."

As for Miss Page's technique, it is not possible to discuss it with even rough justice in this short space. There is a most subtle variation of cadence in accord with the ever-shifting nuances of her thought; and she is almost as fertile an image-maker as Anderson, in this a *virtuoso*. Though more brittle and far less sensuous, she has a sharpness and a fantastic logic all her own, as in "The Stenographers":

> In their eyes I have seen
> The pin men of madness in marathon trim
> race round the track of the stadium pupil.

Dudek's collection is more uneven in quality. Some pieces are rather ordinary fragments of imagism or impressionism. In the majority, however, the simplicity is deceptive. Dudek has that rare gift of the true poet, the ability to savour the most ordinary experience with the freshness of a child and to write about it with the subtlety of an adult. "Mystery you hold me in the nearest atom. . . ." A myopic old woman looking up at a tree, a piece of paper fluttering out of a window, these are transmuted by a kind of self-honesty and a delicate sense of rhythm into a rich emotional experience. His is the poetry of youth, but yet of youth already amused with itself, with the fact that in the spring "even the refuse in the streets looks romantic", and already — because this is mid-twentieth century youth, — meditating on "the idiocy of avarice, of fear, and of the danger of ideals." There is the forthrightness of youth here too, for all the gentleness and grace of the writing. "Let social anger", he writes, "Make ruins in you like an Aztec temple. Be young — But carry an ax of stone to this murderous civilization."

88

Patrick Anderson, though the oldest (31), is perhaps the least disciplined writer of the three. Although he submits himself to sustained functional rhythm, rhyme, assonance and consonance, he is reluctant to discipline his images. They spout like an oil gusher, spread, change colour and at times completely cover the good earth of his meaning. I suspect that Anderson can't scrap an image once he has thought of it, whatever the cost to the over-all intentions of the poem. Unchecked release of metaphor can be justified if one believes in handing over control of a poem to the subconscious, but the very conscious message in Anderson's poems removes him from surrealism and makes it important for him to win the reader to his meaning. Much of his purport, it's true, emerges with re-reading, but some of it lies drowned in the figured foam.

It must be emphasized, however, that such flaws are excesses of a very real strength. No poet in Canada today has given evidence of so bold an imagination, nor been so effective in the epigrammatic and symbolic use of metaphor to convey genuinely mature and important observations on contemporary life. He is also one of the few poets in our recent history who has tackled the theme of Canada itself: Canada, not simply as history or maple leaves or wheat, but as all these and also an enigma in human relations, a national illusion and a mysteriously frustrated promise. His "Poem on Canada", for all that it lacks the feeling of experience of the west, for all its occasional over-simplification of history and disproportionate emphasis upon dear Aunt Hildegarde in England, is one of the most concentrated and sophisticated and thoughtful utterances about this country for many a long day. It is also a poem in image rich and exciting, and in rhythm always accomplished and often deeply moving. . . .

As I Remember
1947: January - March

The new CPM's second issue had certainly been better than the first, and good enough to evoke some gratifying mail. Howard Sergeant, editor of a respected London poetry magazine, *Outposts*, wrote asking for submissions from the four younger poets represented in our December number and proposing an exchange guest-editorship. I agreed gladly; so far as I knew, there had never been an all-Canadian issue of a British magazine.

Patrick Anderson thanked me for my review of his *White Centre*, "a delight after the abysmal amateurishness of most reviews; I am glad that you see that I am rather wide, and hope to achieve a big imaginative and even philosophical sweep one day. The 3 contributions I should like to make to Canadian letters are: 1) formal elegance, intricacy, tension, variety — i.e. more verbal felicity and polish, but not in the merely decorative sense... 2) big architectural structures... with some national and/or regional searching — I have followed at times obvious and derivative *Poem on Canada* with a larger and I think more interesting canvas, still unpublished; 3) a professional criticism, tough, without national favours — the absolute antithesis of Ryerson blurbs, for instance." He went on to complain he was "having quite a struggle for recognition" and blamed it on "a sort of academic conservative conspiracy to ignore anyone new". He had "the awful feeling if one got a Ph.D, joined the Toronto faculty, dined with E.K. Brown and said one was forty-five, one would be a *Canadian Master* ..." I knew how he felt; the same "conspiracy" had delayed my start as a poet and still bothered me at forty-two.

Louis Dudek, now in New York, also wrote me about "the wonderful development of the *Canadian Poetry Magazine*. It is a miracle.... You have changed the magazine into something seriously worth attending to.... John Sutherland wondered whether you could carry the day against the opposition which one must assume is there.... Now, looking at the (last two) issues, I think he would gladly admit that so far you *have*." "So far," but how much farther? Dudek's praise, and his accompanying subscription and five new poems, were the kind of assurance I needed. It was easier, after Dudek's letter, to keep smiling while I read a missive from a stalwart CAAer, Florence Randal Livesay, cancelling her subscription: "I disliked very much Gustafson and Ford.... I could not find anyone who understood the poems among all my poet-friends including Helena Coleman. Why should we be forced to read them twice?... a disservice to the magazine to use extreme modern verse. . . ." And something from Leo Cox, another favourite poetaster of the CAA (he was supposed to be helping Pat Waddington, my Montreal representative, get poems from the young French) objecting to my publishing Anderson's poem "Nuns" because it upset his Catholic wife. These were the sort of letters which made me have second thoughts about my own editorial in the December issue, in which I was affirming the existence of a natural "poetic understanding in the common people".

From Mona Cannon, O'Brien's secretary, I got a letter which both warmed and disturbed me. "The speed with which you have rejuvenated CPM is what is known as a miracle; a couple of months ago it was gasping for breath." But she went on to break the news she was resigning because of overwork. The CAA have two fulltime office girls but Deacon won't let them help her. And she can no longer put up with her pennypinching employer. Despite the big increase in subscriptions we are only "holding our own"; O'Brien has failed to appoint CPM representatives across the country, as requested by the CAA, and won't advertise or even put the magazines on the stands because the dealers send back soiled ones.

I wanted to grab a plane and descend on Toronto and O'Brien, but the travel expenses at that time equalled a month of my UBC salary. I could react best by increasing activity at the Vancouver end. I made up an evening of poetry readings from work published in the last two issues and canvassed local cultural groups by phone; by this means we got a sizable number of subscriptions from members of the Vancouver Institute and the University Women's Club. I soothed O'Brien with a letter agreeing to his reduction of the author payment-rate to ten cents a line and attached my draft of an advertisement announcing a new long Pratt poem to come. I took a day off to search and find three newsstand outlets for CPM. Esther and I fired off review copies to scores of magazines in North America and Britain. I drew up a standard letter and promotional material and a list of possible donors or fifty-dollar "life subscribers" in B.C. and Esther mailed it out. We got the March copy off before February ended. It pleased me to notice that nine of the contributors were under thirty years of age, and two of them over seventy.

At the last moment I found time to include a review of Robert Finch.

1947

The Poems of Robert Finch

review; *Canadian Poetry Magazine*, March 1947.

After long delay, the Oxford University Press presents the first collection of the work of Professor Finch, of the Department of Modern Languages in the University of Toronto. His poems provide serious competition to the three Ryerson Press poets reviewed in our last issue, for the Governor-General's Award.

No other poet in Canada can rival Finch as a formal duellist in words. For him the dimeter couplet is a stiletto of irony, free verse a sinuous rapier, and the sonnet a damascened sword, . . . symmetrical, pointed, etched minutely with curious and yet controlled figures. . . . Finch is an accomplished musician and painter, and in his best work every sound, every particle of an idea, is chosen with almost finicky care to achieve a singly audible-visible effect. The result is only rarely "precious" or merely decorative; predominantly it is poetry of the suavest subtlety, the expression of a mind nimble but mature, of a character quietly honest, sensitive, knowing, and most courteously independent — a personality in the best sense "civilized."

Without being in any sense an imitator, he can match Empson or Sitwell in the single image that grows like a tree throughout a poem, lifting branches precise with symbols for our time. And, despite the gulfs of difference, there are bridges of kinship with Housman, both in impeccability and deceitful simplicity of form, and in the wry epicureanism of thought, the tendency to "train for ill" in the hope that good, if it come, will carry the added delight of surprise. It is with Wallace Stevens and the French *Symbolistes*, however, that the ties are perhaps closest, in Finch's delicate analysis of the protean illusions of the heart, in the irony of his humanitarianism, the simultaneous treasuring of independence and of friendship, the almost despairing groping through the long "miles from heart to head."

For all the cosmopolitan quality, the echoes of Oriental painting, the Gallic fastidiousness, the climax of his success is the composing of these most diverse elements into poetry based on the Canadian scene, on an Etobicoke river in hazelnut season, the rush-hour along College Street, Toronto, or a smalltown station platform. This is not to say that Finch is a "native" poet, after all, in Smith's terminology, but that he brings his continentalism home. He is, in fact, very un-Canadian in his hatred of the cheap, and his devotion to the world of taste and art. And yet perhaps in his guarded frankness and almost diffident assertion of the virtues of hope and endurance, he is part of the best of us.

As I Remember
1947: April - September

With the end of spring term UBC came before CPM. My first western Writers' Workshop was graduating. Most of the twenty were heading into teaching or domesticity or some well-protected harbour like law; but there were two or three who just wanted to write. How to help them keep from starving while they learned to make a living with words? There was little I could do for this first crop, but I had laid plans which would bear fruit in a year's time. I'd been impressed with the reputation of Iowa State University's creative writing program which included even graduate courses leading to a Master of Fine Arts degree, and had begun a correspondence with Paul Engle, the director, sending him some material from our workshop. He replied encouragingly and urged me to put up my best students in the spring of '48 for teaching fellowships in the Iowa graduate school. The result was that Harlow went to Iowa City that fall, stayed several years, and came back to B.C. with a wife and an MFA. Master of Fuck All, Harlow said the orthodox American professors called it, and indeed it was difficult to know how he could use such a degree, still exotic in the Fifties, to snare a job back in Canada. However, I'd been putting lines out to the National Film Board and the Canadian Broadcasting Corporation, and one of these connected for Harlow. He joined the local CBC station as an assistant talks producer, and worked up eventually to Station Manager.

In a February session of my writers' class discussing "freedom of the press", we discovered that one of the students had a brother in the book distribution business, and the brother had a copy of the federal government's secret list of books currently banned from entry into Canada. The ban was being applied under the authority of a little-known section in the Customs Act which established an anonymous Examiner of Customs with sweeping powers to stop at the border and return or destroy any printed or artistic matter deemed by him to be "obscene, blasphemous, immoral, seditious or treasonable". It seemed to us that such a list needed a public airing, at least. By means I never inquired into, my student brought me a photocopy of the list the next day.

It was a shocker; there was at least one book on it by Balzac, Farrell, Faulkner, Joyce, Henry Miller (all), Mailer, Maupassant, Margaret Sanger, Trotsky, Edmund Wilson, and so on. When I showed the list to Sedgewick and other English colleagues I discovered that none of them knew it existed. A lawyer found me the relevant clauses in the

Customs Act, warned me I might be in danger of legal process by circulating what might be a stolen document, and advised me to seek revision of the Act through my Parliamentary representative. Though my MP was not the sort likely to champion anything but the *status quo*, I included him in a roster of a dozen or more parliamentarians to whom I now sent copies of the list with a letter of appeal. I got only polite acknowledgements from him and all the others except for John Diefenbaker. He was only a back-bencher at this time, but he proved to be then, as throughout his life, an alert guardian of the sovereignty of Parliament. It was to be several years before Ottawa revised the *Customs Act* sufficiently to replace the anonymous Examiner with an identifiable committee responsible to the House, and to ensure that the right of a Canadian to import any given item of print was one that could be decided ultimately in a Canadian court of law. Back in '47, I kept writing and sending lists to authors and representatives of the press and radio, urging them to make a public issue of the customs ban.

The authors proved, at first, as shy of the issue as the politicians. Among the exceptions were Robertson Davies and Roderick Haig-Brown. At this time I hadn't met either of them but I had read *The Diary of Samuel Marchbanks* and *A River Never Sleeps* the previous year, both with intense enjoyment, the latter with the extra-literary pleasure of an amateur naturalist and a fellow-angler. Haig-Brown wrote promising to publicize the issue as much as he could without compromising his position as the stipendiary magistrate of Campbell River. It was not until 1950, however, that the two of us were able to plan a joint talk on the subject to the Vancouver Civil Liberties Association. This had been arranged by Duncan Macnair, Dorothy Livesay's husband; Haig-Brown was the tenth person Duncan had approached to share the platform with me. The others were all newspapermen who found themselves otherwise engaged, and indeed at the last minute Haig-Brown phoned that he could not come because of a magistrate's court that day. The press continued to offer me a stone wall of silence until 1949, when Pierre Berton got *Maclean's* interested. The CBC also lowered its barriers in 1949 (allowing me to raise the issue tangentially in a talk on Joyce's *Ulysses*, which appears later in this book).

By the end of March '47 I was once more tangled in the mare's nest of CPM. The resignation of the reliable and sympathetic Mrs. Cannon was a blow to me, though one which might have been softened if it had led to CPM's paid secretary being someone living in Vancouver. O'Brien, however, quickly appointed a Toronto high school graduate with no experience in editing and whose published verse gave me no promise she would like what I was publishing. There were to my knowledge at least two intelligent young people in Toronto with both secretarial experience and enthusiasm for the new CPM: Mrs. Gertrude

Garbutt and Miss Elizabeth Campbell. Both of them had already volunteered when they knew Mrs. Cannon was resigning but O'Brien had rebuffed them without even informing me. While I was writing him about this, the first copies of the March CPM arrived, as usual belatedly and with numerous proof errors committed after I had returned the galleys.

My frustrations were increased by a reply from E.K. Brown in Chicago to a letter I had sent him inquiring why he had not mentioned CPM in his annual survey of Canadian literature. Brown wrote me it was because he had received no copies of CPM since I had taken over editorship — this despite my specific request to O'Brien that "Letters in Canada" continue to receive copies. A few days later I heard from Northrop Frye that he too was not receiving his CPM's, and I banged off another letter of complaint to O'Brien (to which he never replied). The next day I received from Deacon a photocopy of an illuminating letter he had sent to O'Brien ticking him off for bugging him with problems that the Management Board was supposed to handle. Furthermore, went on the President of the CAA, it was O'Brien's job, not Deacon's, to compose any "begging letters" on behalf of the magazine, send out publicity, secure advertising and develop circulation. If O'Brien felt he needed assistance or advice he should add to his Management Board the businessmen whose names Deacon had given him and who had volunteered their aid. The letter made it evident to me for the first time that O'Brien was proving as much a plague in the Toronto office as he was to me in Vancouver.

I now decided to go over O'Brien's head and make a series of demands to the Management Board itself.

1. That CPM be placed and maintained on Toronto newsstands. I pointed out that in six months I had personally placed sixty copies of each issue on Vancouver stalls, where there had been none before.

2. That CPM be regularly advertised across Canada.

3. That a member of the Board undertake a national circulation drive. I mentioned that my volunteer aides in Vancouver had now doubled the number of B.C. subscribers.

4. That another member of the Board organize a drive for Donors.

5. That a Vancouver member be added to the Board. I suggested Professor William Robbins of the UBC English Department, and that Northrop Frye be asked to join the Board in Toronto.

6. That a duplicate of the card index of CPM subscribers, made for me without charge by the UBC Registrar, be established in O'Brien's office and kept up to date.

7. That my associate editor in Toronto, Charles Bruce, an experienced journalist, and not O'Brien, be placed in charge of final proofing.

While waiting for a reply to this blast I completed assembling the June issue. The big item was a new long poem by Pratt, running near to a thousand lines. O'Brien had been resisting its publication — "the magazine needs space for other CAA members who are being rejected; we could run an extract and save for them" — but Deacon, in his letter to me, had agreed it should be run in entirety and specially advertised in advance. "You will never have anything to sell that is more likely to sell," Deacon had written O'Brien. Even if I had lacked Pratt's poem I had now enough good material to fill this and the next issue. I wrote Pat Waddington that he no longer needed to hunt for Montreal poetry, unless it was in French. He had had no luck with the *Canadien* poets, though he had solicited many of them with the support of my French colleagues from International Service days, Gérard Arthur and René Garneau. They had approached Alain Grandbois, Rina Lasnier and Robert Choquette without success. The only poem so far volunteered in the French language was from Jovette Bernier which we had to reject because it had already been published.

Whether it was spring or the laws of chance, the affairs of CPM took a turn for the better in April. The news came that Finch's poems, which I had praised so highly in our March issue, had won the Governor General's medal. Lawren Harris dropped into my office one day with a donation of fifty dollars and a promise to approach the Vancouver Arts Council for support of CPM. Mrs. Cannon wrote that she hoped to find time to rejoin the Toronto office soon. "Don't give up — but make Management do the publicity and find the dollars". And my old undergraduate friend Dal Grauer, by now the president of the B.C. Electric Company, was one of three that month who sent us fifty-dollar life subscriptions.

Submissions were now coming in steadily along with both new and renewal subscriptions, and a great number of fan letters. Some that were censorious were equally heart-warming for me. A Mr. Edwin Gardner-Smith, introducing himself as "a representative of the ordinary, well-educated, mill-run of readers", wrote me that I had turned CPM into something "repugnant alike to the eye and the ear . . . a Canadian Prose Magazine whose contents need a stethescope or x-ray apparatus to discover the meaning". He found only one poem he liked; it was by D.C. Scott, "a gem which ushers us reverently through the portals of Nature into the very presence of the Triune God!" Everything else I had published was either "modernistic or futuristic or whatever kind of istic".

My letters to my Toronto managers were also having an effect of sorts. Financial control was shifted from O'Brien to Dr. Jacob Markowitz, a well-known Toronto surgeon and self-styled literary patron. I had got to know "Marko" in the *Forum* days and knew him to be a highly energetic man with a great desire to be helpful. I thought him given as well to manic enthusiasms and consequently, when he wrote me in May that CPM's "finances were secured", I took it as meaning no more than that we were not yet bankrupt. In any case we got the June number out in May.

Among the books I reviewed for this issue was one which set me thinking about certain lacks in even the best of contemporary Canadian poetry. It was the new edition of the *Oxford Book of Australasian Verse*. I felt that the best of its contents showed a vigour and a humanism beyond what we were used to. Australians, though not New Zealanders, seemed to have drawn on a more colourful and original popular speech. Or was it that Canadian poets were still being too genteel to exploit properly the Canadian popular idiom? Even in the nineteenth century, Australian poets were more tough-minded than ours, less routinely patriotic or pious or sentimental. We were perhaps more pacific and ironic, but also more stuffy, more bucolic but less indigenous.

May brought me a release again from lectures and incidentally posed a new professorial question for me, a pleasant one. Several of my first batch of graduated writers, the ones who were staying in Vancouver for the summer, came to tell me they wanted not only to go on writing but to keep together, for the time being at least, as a group. They wanted to benefit from each other's criticism and, if possible, mine. I leapt at this chance to form a social-literary club, for I well knew that I would benefit equally from their company and criticism. So began Authors Anonymous. It was to last for many years, with constant losings and freshenings of membership, and the inclusion from time to time of established writers who had never gone near a creative writing class. Among the latter were Eric Nicol and Ethel Wilson. It was the latter indeed who was later very often our hostess and who read us the first draft of *Swamp Angel*. Out of town visitors who were writers or editors were often brought along to evenings and in this way I met for the first time Roderick Haig-Brown, fresh and tanned from guiding salmon-fishers that morning in the Gulf of Georgia. I remember too John Gray, the warm-hearted, shrewd editor at Toronto Macmillan, talking in nervous jets between whackings of his pipe and growing red-faced with anecdotal glee.

That was the spring too when I renewed my campaign to improve the contemporary poetry holdings in the UBC library. I was not teaching any of the courses in modern literature, but my writer-students needed the stimulus of many more twentieth-century books than they could afford to buy or that any library in B.C. contained — Pound's early *Cantos*, for example, and indeed most modern American poetry. I drew up *desiderata* for the librarian, searched the second-hand stores, appealed to literary clubs for gift copies, and badgered Larry MacKenzie to allot more money to the campus library. It was not wasted effort, and led to the coming of a new and more contemporary-minded librarian to UBC

In May I met a writer who was to affect my own activities for some time afterwards. At the University of Toronto in the Thirties I had managed to persuade the English Department to accept from one of my students, in lieu of an academic thesis for the M.A., a book-length group of original short stories. My protegée, Sybil Hutchinson, had written some very able and vivid recreations of rural characters and doings in the Point Pelée district of Ontario, some of which were later published in Canadian journals. If there had been a Canada Council at that time, she would undoubtedly have received the financial aid she needed to continue, and might be ranked today among our leading novelists. Instead, she took on routine jobs in editorial offices until, by '47, she had risen to be Jack McClelland's first and very dedicated editor-in-chief. Sybil understood that my contractual relations with Ryerson prevented me from submitting my poetry to McClelland and Stewart, but she also knew that I had some potential Canadian authors in my workshop looking for publishers, and that I hoped myself to write a somewhat ribald novel about the war I'd been in. So she took pains to read and comment on the stories of McConnell and others I thought worth her attention, and made sure I was supplied with any good new novel that came the way of "M&S". Earlier that spring she had sent me *Bonheur d'Occasion* and so made me aware of a new and most accomplished French-Canadian writer, Gabrielle Roy. Now she sent me another novel by a writer I'd never heard of. This was *Under the Volcano*, by Malcolm Lowry.

I had scarcely finished devouring it with amazement and excitement, and was about to begin a second reading, when a letter came from Lowry himself, telling me he too was living in a shack not thirty miles from mine, and that Sybil Hutchinson had sent him my address. He and his wife Margerie would like to meet the Birneys.

It was a meeting that led among other things to my being, in the Sixties, joint compiler and editor, with Margerie, of Lowry's literary remains, as well as agent for his poems. He, in turn, was to read *Turvey* the next year in manuscript and to write the first and one of the most appreciative reviews of that book I ever got. Mention of all this would have little relevance here if it were not that Lowry, from the time I met him to his death, maintained he was "a Canadian writer" Indeed some Canadian critics still want to claim him.*

In June Vancouver was the scene of the annual convention of the CAA. I was required to report on my first year of CPM editing to a

---

*A full account of my association with Lowry will appear in *Dylan Thomas and Malcolm Lowry in Vancouver*, scheduled for publication by McClelland & Stewart in Toronto, early in 1981.

"business meeting". I recall that the predominant faces wore either impersonal masks of CAA executives or the hostile stares of old guard poets whom I had failed to publish. I was able to say that we had, in the four issues, printed verse by sixty-eight Canadians and reviews by ten. Some of the former were domiciled in other countries, one being our ambassador to the USSR (R.A.D. Ford). I noted that men and women were almost equally represented, that ten percent of them were over fifty years of age, and thirty-five percent in their twenties — several of these appearing in print for the first time. On the other hand, most of the better-known Canadian poets had been represented; what's more, many of these had never appeared before in CPM. As a result of this gratifying aid from the poets themselves, I said, and from new supporters of the magazine in British Columbia, subscription and book-store sales had more than doubled. These gains, however, had been offset by a major rise in printing costs (from $365 to $988), due in part to our having increased our run to thirteen hundred copies. To keep peace in the family, if possible, I gave all the credit to O'Brien (who was not at the conference) for securing new advertising, which he was actually at last doing. However, for generous and unpaid general assistance my thanks went first to my wife Esther and my CW students in Vancouver, and in Toronto to Gertrude Garbutt and Mona Cannon.

The CAA conference proved lively at only one session and that in a sick sort of way. It was when the Governor General's medal for poetry was presented *in absentia* to Robert Finch. The proceedings were opened by Bill Deacon who called upon one of the stuffed owls of the Association, the portly John Murray Gibbon (author of *Hearts and Faces* and *Pagan Love* and other soggy pot-boilers of the Twenties), to make the presentation. Mr. Finch, said Deacon, — rather casually, I thought — had informed the Association he was unable to attend, so he was asking Mr. Birney to "speak *briefly*" in acceptance of the medal on Finch's behalf. I had been looking around for Finch and was stunned by this last-minute warning that I was to be his proxy.

For the next twenty minutes the audience listened to a rambling address by Gibbon on the virtues of the Victorian poets, followed by an outright attack on Finch's book and indirectly on my favourable review of it in CPM. Professor Finch, said Gibbon, was a fake; he could not even rhyme properly, something even illiterate writers of folksongs know how to do. The trouble with university poets and some so-called editors, he said, was they had no ear. Gibbon then proceeded to read out with earnest scorn various sonnets of Finch, in which indeed there was nowhere a "true" rhyme — for the excellent reason, which Gibbon had patently never considered, that Finch was carefully chiming with half-rhymes. Nevertheless, despite this display of ignorance and bad manners, his attack drew solid applause from

100

most of the CAA-ers assembled. Then Deacon called me up, tapping his wristwatch at me as I neared the platform.

I was too angry and too pressed to be an effective rebutter. I tried to explain assonance, and I defended Finch's artistry. The applause for this was what reporters call scattered, though in one corner I was happy to see Duncan Macnair's big hands beating each other powerfully, and thought I heard him shouting "Up yours, you old Canada Goose."

The full hypocrisy and double-dealing that led to this event, however, did not become clear to me until I posted Finch his medal along with a description of the award ceremony. Robert replied that the G-G must surely be "the world's most mysteriously presented decoration . . . because, apart from what has appeared in the papers I have never received a communication from anyone on the matter until your present letter". In other words both Deacon and Gibbon had plotted the scene beforehand. It was embarrassing enough for the CAA brass (who appointed the personnel of each Governor-General's Award Committee) to have "twice honoured me", as Deacon had written me when he appointed me editor of the Association's magazine, only to see me exclude almost all the CAA's favourite bards from its pages. It was worse now to see the next award go to some unknown French professor who hadn't even joined the Association. My guess was that Gibbon had demanded from Deacon that the convention disavow any apparent approval of Finch's book and reassure the main body of CAA versifiers their verses would be restored to favour. Deacon, I was sure, did not want as yet to fire me and lose the new youth support I was bringing to CAA. But his interest in poetic quality was minimal. He wanted to build and keep and lead as big an authors' power-group as possible. So he played the medal-giving down the middle, "forgot" to invite Finch, let Gibbon lead an Old Guard attack, then trapped me into a stopwatched extempore rebuttal.

After the conference I fled to "Lieben", Einar Neilson's cliff-house retreat on Bowen Island, and spent the rest of the summer there finishing a new book of poems, *The Strait of Anian*, and making an outline and first chapter for Sybil Hutchinson of my projected novel, *Turvey*. I had of course also to keep up with CPM correspondence and assemble the September number. On weekends Esther brought me the mail, which was as usual both swings and roundabouts. There was a note from Anne Marriott resigning from the editorial board by reason of marriage and removal to the wilds of Prince George. But there was also a lovely set of poems which Frank Scott had persuaded Pat Page to send me; she had been holding back for over a year because of her settled dislike of the CAA.

So long as I wanted to edit CPM, of course, I could not afford to break clean with the CAA, which owned it. I still remember a lovely sunny day on that Gulf Island when I had to leave a poem half done and take ferry and bus into Vancouver to be present at something the local CAA was calling a Round Table. The occasion was the reading of her poems by a travelling *diseuse* from an eastern branch to a dozen grim old ladies in the overstuffed and sunless home of a local patron of the arts. It was a singular performance; the lady had studied elocution and wore black tights and an ermine cloak. I remember wishing her verses were half as exciting as her legs; but her audience seemed delighted by the rhymes, and, at least politely, unaware of the gams.

I went into town another and happier time to arrange a welcoming party at the Birneys' Acadia shack for Sybil Hutchinson. She had come west for the first time, in search of publishable manuscripts for McClelland & Stewart. At the party she met Bill and Alice McConnell, who had both by now written a considerable body of largely unpublished fiction, and Malcolm and Margerie Lowry. Sybil bore away one of Bill's novels and two of Lowry's short stories set in B.C. Malcolm told her he wanted them published first in Canada but, as Sybil wrote me, where? He needed money for them, but the Canadian magazines which would be glad to have them, such as *Northern Review* and *The Forum*, paid nothing. Maclean's would pay but didn't want them. This was the situation now anywhere in Canada, Sybil wrote me later, for short fiction of quality. On her way back from Vancouver she had visited Professor Salter's Advanced Composition class at the University of Alberta and learned that he regularly advised his short story writers to try American journals first. It was advice which one of them, Robert Blackburn had already taken with some success. A story he could not place in Canada had been accepted by the *Atlantic Monthly*.

In the September CPM we came out at last with a poem in French. It was by Simone Routier, a Montreal poet who had already published collections in both Canada and France. The issue also marked the first appearance in any Canadian magazine of a poem derived from a radio script — the final chorus of Lister Sinclair's "Ill-met by moonlight". I still think it one of the best poems written for that medium. (I had got to know Lister in those first years after the war, and owe it partly to him that I was encouraged later to write radio drama myself.) The issue was also the first in Canada to publish a poem by Malcolm Lowry; it was one of his best, "Sestina in a Cantina", as fine a piece of writing, to my taste, as anything in the *Volcano*.

Among the reviews I wrote for this issue was a brief one on a new selection of Lampman's poems by D.C. Scott. Re-reading Lampman confirmed me in thinking him the finest literary artist in nineteenth century Canada, a wise, gentle and perfectly honest writer, cut off while still maturing. I found it interesting to review a new book by D.C. Scott himself at the same time, his *Circle of Affection*. Scott, a kindred spirit to Lampman but more fortunate, was still publishing new work, at the age of eighty-four, more precise and delicate than ever, in form as in feeling.

Dorothy Livesay's *Poems for People* also came to me for review in the September number. I thought the title inapt since most of the poems in it were specifically directed to children, but I considered the book as a whole marked an increase both in warmth and in discipline. There was now in her work a brooding compassion which her control of word and cadence prevented from dropping into sentimentality; by the same token her social protests had become less stark, less doctrinaire, allowing us to feel for man's need, beyond subsistence, for mutual tolerance and affection.

When I began my second year as CPM's improbable editor I was greatly cheered by a sheaf of clippings Gertrude Garbutt sent me: reviews from leading eastern Canadian newspapers praising the magazine. "The new editorial staff, displaying initiative and vitality, has vastly improved the quality" *(Ottawa Evening Journal)*. "Discovers new talent" *(Montreal Standard)*. Deacon himself, in the Toronto *Globe & Mail*, declared that "in a new idiom and new forms, the magazine flourishes anew". There was even a puff from the New York League to Support Poetry. Best was a whole editorial by Sandwell in his *Saturday Night* noting "the immense improvement... during the year... especially in point of originality and willingness to experiment, and the magazine has almost completely got away from the merely imitative and nostalgic."

The Representative Canadian Poet Today

Radio script for broadcast to Britain over the International Service of the CBC; 23 October, 1947.

Who are the new Canadian poets? Where do they live, and how? What sort of things do they write and why? Are they any good?... These are only half the questions I was asked to answer in these three minutes. A statistical approach seemed the only possible one, so I wrote down the names of all actively-writing Canadian poets who seem to me to be worth reading, and who had a book out or nearly out. By a charitable process of selection, I got 28 names. Reading these over, I can proceed to several generalizations, probably none of them of any consequence, but perhaps a little surprising to any who are still thinking of Canadian poetry in terms of sonnets about maple trees. All but one of my 28 poets are city-dwellers; nine live in Toronto, six in Vancouver, four in Montreal, and so on. Treated as a composite figure, this living Canadian poet is three-quarters male, was born in Canada about thirty-five years ago, has moved around the country a good deal and is definitely not a regionalist. He likes to consider himself an internationalist both culturally and politically, is very gloomy about the state of our times and inclined to be satirical about established ideas and institutions (though he is rarely humorous). It is true that, of my 28, two or three might best be described as belated Georgians and Imagists, one is primarily a narrative writer (some say the best narrative poet now writing in the English language) and one is a radio verse dramatist. But the great majority are so-called "metaphysical" poets, philosophical and a little crabbed, showing the influence of Eliot, Hopkins, Auden. You will notice that English influences still loom larger than American, though one occasionally sees the shadow of the long beard of Walt Whitman.

And this brings us to what is perhaps the worst thing we have to say about our composite Canadian poet today. He hasn't much of a style or attitude of his own. He is so anxious to be a contemporary and to speak to the world about the world's problems, that he avoids the kind of local topic or reference or idiom which might mark him as a nationalist in a time when nationalism is suspect. Perhaps also, the younger Canadian poet is anxious to be in fashion, and still suffering a little from the Colonial Complex. He has turned to sprung rhythms, jazz dissonances, half-rhymes, etc., not because he personally felt the need of them but because in England and America they are now the thing.

But the real question, the one I haven't answered: is he any good, this Canadian poet? Here statistical silhouettes are of no help to me. I don't know. Good for what? Good for Canadian poetry? Certainly. It was high time we laid away our Victorian metrical antimacassars. Good for the world? Perhaps, since poets who are internationalists will presumably not incite to massacre. But good, good in comparison, with, well let's have it, with British poets? I suggest you get hold of our poetry and be the judge. I don't think we have produced anyone as creative as Auden, as original as Dylan Thomas, or as influential as Eliot. But we have a second-string, if you like which I suspect is as good as your own and, if proportions of population are considered, perhaps even a little better. Certainly I am prepared to argue that the *Canadian Poetry Magazine,* which I edit, is as sound and contemporary a quarterly of verse as any now appearing in England. You may object that in this matter I am sure to be prejudiced. True. As a matter of fact I even counted myself among the 28 best Canadian poets today — so you can see I've been unreliable from the start.

As I Remember

1947 (November) - 1948 (February)

When it became known that applications for my second creative writing workshop, in the fall of 1947, totalled over a hundred, my colleagues in the English Department were variously surprised, amused, or annoyed, according to their natures. Some felt such popularity proved how low my standards were. I argued, somewhat weakly, that there were a thousand more arts seniors who had *not* applied. A better defense was that my class of twenty was picked beforehand from a scrutiny of submitted material; consequently, if anyone failed, it would be because I had failed in my judgement, or because (as was the case of the only failure the previous year) the student (now a prominent B.C. journalist and editor) simply wrote nothing. Flushed with my own arguments I then went to Sedgewick and asked for a second workshop class, preferably at the first year level. He wanted to say yes but we both knew the Dean would say no because it would increase our budget, so he spoke to the Dean and the Dean said no.

The new class was a delight. One of those twenty I still count among my dearest friends, John Wardroper, is today an editor of the *Sunday Times* and the author of several books on art history. Also registered was an ex-bomber pilot, James Jackson, who began a dramatic novel for me about his nightmare flights over Japanese-occupied Java during World War II. In this class too, or the next — I write from memory — was Norman Klenman, soon to be a film-maker; two bright young news-men, Bill Galt (later the managing editor of the Vancouver *Sun*) and shy, witty "Gem" Mortimer, already a contributor to *Punch*; Bob Harlow and Ernie Perrault (now well-known west coast novelists); Phil and Hilda Thomas (today the "grandparents" of the Vancouver folk-song community); and Paul Wright who, after a session at Iowa's graduate school, would return to Canada and a career as a writer-producer for the CBC.

Some of the short stories developing that fall in my CW class were so promising that I wrote Sybil Hutchinson proposing to edit for McClelland and Stewart a collection called "Canada West Today", which would have a story by each of a number of my students over the previous two years as well as writing by more established B.C. authors. I had confirmed that I could get fresh fiction from Livesay, Floris McLaren, Haig-Brown, Ethel Wilson, Malcolm Lowry, Eric Nicol (his first serious short story, "The Mink"), and possibly Emily Carr. I was surprised myself at what a strong regional anthology might be mustered now in B.C. However, Sybil replied that her firm was already committed to a collection projected by A.J.M. Smith, to be called "New Canadian Writing". She asked me to wait till this was out and meantime suggested that, to have the title I proposed, my collection should be expanded to include work by prominent Albertans like Henry Kreisel and such graduates of Salter's workshop as Blackburn, Christine van der Mark and W.O. Mitchell. By December it was clear that M&S now regarded any book of short stories as a sure loser, and a regional western one as a certain disaster. I got further discouragement from other Toronto publishers and eventually dropped the idea.

This was the autumn when CPM's poets began to get a hearing outside Canada. In October I was invited to the University of Washington by its English Department and the editors of *Poetry Northwest* to lecture on contemporary Canadian poetry. The invitation was in part the result of my having arranged an "exchange subscription" between our magazines, as by now we had done with several other North American journals. My "lecture" was mainly a reading of poems which we had printed in CPM (by Pratt, Anderson, Livesay, Finch, Smith and Dudek). It was picked up and broadcast over a Seattle station and was probably the first "media" breakthrough for Canadian poetry in the western states. This led me later to make a good number of similar readings on other American campuses. In October my old employer, the CBC International Service in Montreal, asked me for a thumbnail report on "the new Canadian poet" (which follows), and that in turn led to my giving Charles Wasserman a forty-minute interview on the Canadian poets' "revolt against traditionalism"; it was broadcast to Britain. And I was now assured that the London *Outpost's* Canadian number I was beginning to assemble would appear in the coming year.

Apart frim the usual editorial pressures, like getting the December issue out in November, and the unusual one of assembling the contents and writing an introduction for the special Canadian number of London *Outposts*, the rest of 1947 passed in professorial routines beyond the world of CanLit. There was a pleasant exception in December when I persuaded Sybil Hutchinson to consider a first book of poems by Roy Daniells, now my colleague at UBC, for the new M&S "Indian File" series, and I helped him to prepare the manuscript. It was accepted in January and I was happy to write the "promo" for the jacket.

By January the main contents of the March CPM had reached me from Howard Sergeant in London. I was glad to see what a wide variety of British poets he had selected and that he had included many who were under thirty years of age. I felt the issue would be a landmark — the first time a Canadian magazine had devoted an entire issue to contemporary British poetry. Only the reviews would be Canadian. Among the pile of books waiting for notice, I spotted *Sarah Binks*, and exercised the Editor's privilege to review it myself.

1948

Required Reading for the CAA

A review of P.G. Hiebert's *Sarah Binks; Canadian Poetry Magazine*, March 1948

It has remained for a professor of chemistry in the University of Manitoba to write the first funny book about Canadian poetry and to supply a local habitation and a name for that protean nymph, the Bad Canadian Poetess.

As Dr. Hiebert tells it, the life story of his imagined Sarah Binks, W.P.M. (Wheat Pool Medal), L.L.D. (posthumously awarded by St. Midget's College), the Sweet Songstress of Saskatchewan and the Poet's Poetess, is a "documented" satire... on our tendency to find literary swans in every village goose.

In a style that carefully parodies the pedantries of academic criticism, Dr. Hiebert traces the career of the simple country girl from Willows, Saskatchewan, who, "unschooled and unspoiled..., captured in her net of poesy the flatness of that great province." She first rises to fame through tender verses in *The Horsebreeder's Gazette* and *Swine & Kine* (examples are quoted and lovingly analyzed). Later, her art is intellectually enriched by contact with an old geology textbook belonging to Wm. Greenglow, the local school teacher (failed B.A.) — "he had the educator's peculiar genius for imparting knowledge without himself assimilating it" — and given emotional depth through contact with Henry Welkin, the binder salesman with whom she made her one and only excursion from Willows. With him she spent a vaguely footnoted two weeks amid the glitter and allure of the Athens of Saskatchewan — Regina. When Henry fades ambiguously from the scene, Sarah returns to her native alkali and goes through her "Dark Hour".

But she recovers to sing gaily once more of the Spring, as in her beautiful "Spreading Time", or with fortitude of the Winter:

> Beyond the dripping nose and tear,
> Beyond the chilblain and the bite,
> Beyond the scratchy underwere,
> Beyond the eighty-below at night,
> There still must lie — though drifts conceal —
> Some hidden good for man's descry,
> Some secret bounty for his weal,
> Which man should shovel out — or try.

We should have thousands more of such gems if Sarah had not accidentally bitten into a horse thermometer and swallowed a full tablespoonful of mercury. That will serve as an example of Sarah's style, or I should say, of her creator's finesse in building and toppling rhythms and rhymes and meaning. He has produced something uncannily like the real bad verse written in all seriousness by scores of aspiring bards every year in this bardic country of ours.

The hundred or more ditties of this kind which Dr. Hiebert has sprinkled through his "biography" probably constitute a larger body of metrical burlesque than can be found in all the rest of Canadian literature. These and the whole book are recommended reading for anyone with a sense of humour, and required reading for all English professors, reviewers, and members of the Canadian Authors' Association.

As I Remember

1948 March - June

March saw the beginning of the end of my CPM editorship. For two months now I'd been getting no replies from O'Brien or his secretary to my letters, no quarterly fifty-dollar stipend, no submissions or subscriptions forwarded, no comment on either the December or March numbers, no mail at all except for proofs and copies. In contrast, an increasing amount of fan-mail and favourable press notices for these issues was coming addressed directly to me. Then from Mrs. Garbutt and other Toronto supporter-friends I began to get warnings there was some sort of boycott afoot among CAA old-timers in Toronto and Montreal, an organized plot to sabotage my editorship, a mass withdrawal of subscriptions, headed by traditionalist versifiers whose work I had rejected. I consulted with my associate editors and helpers, and to forestall a useless confrontation we agreed on a joint resignation. This was sent to Deacon and quickly accepted; he notified me that Arthur Bourinot would replace me after the June issue (most of which I had already prepared). On the heels of this came a letter from CPM's major donor, my friend Dr. Markowitz; it was the first he had written me. Its contents may be gathered from my reply:

Dear Marko,

Your compliments about the March [British] issue I have passed on to its editor, Mr. Howard Sergeant. I am glad that at least one issue of the magazine under my editorship was pleasing to you.

You write: 'Do you know that we've had 300 cancellations of subscriptions, many of them accompanied by a note that they were out of sympathy with your taste in selecting poems?' No, Marko, I did not know this, and I should be interested to see the actual figures and, particularly, these letters. [I never did.]

And now I will ask you some questions. Did you know that I have repeatedly asked O'Brien & M_____ to keep me informed of circulation figures and that they have ignored my requests? Did you know that this is part of a general policy of making it tough for me, originating among the disappointed poetasters in the Toronto branch? Did you know that I have *never* been sent a single letter, or received a letter, from a subscriber cancelling a subscription *for any reason*? Do you know that I could produce 300 letters myself from my editorial files, letters from writers and others all over Canada and some from abroad, saying how much they think the magazine had improved under my editorship? And do you remember that when I agreed, reluctantly, to take over the moribund CPM I warned you and others connected with it that we would lose some subscribers but gain as many others? And this is what has happened.

If the CAA Exec. had replaced the senile Mr. O'Brien with a business manager with some notion of tact and some understanding of how to increase circulation — as I requested more than once — and if the appointment of a Circulation Assistant hadn't been postponed until it was too late, we would still be expanding in circulation despite the dropping-off of rhymesters who used to subscribe to CPM in Kirkconnell's days because he published their wretched verse. I could a tale unfold... but you don't ask for it. I don't blame you for being worried about circulation, since it is your generosity that has been imposed on to keep CPM afloat. And naturally you have heard O'Brien's story and not my side of it. However, I feel no need to justify myself to you. The notices CPM has received in the press, the letters I have had from people of consequence in the literary scene in Canada, console me for one of the most unpleasant experiences in human relations I have had to subject myself to. I refer to the necessity to carry on correspondence weekly with a man as stupid, inefficient, cantankerous and hostile as Mr. A.H. O'Brien. If you really want to improve CPM, I suggest you begin by firing O'Brien and pensioning off [his secretary] who was appointed, by the way, over my protests.

Finally, I find your remark that 'a poet is not the best judge of poetry, which is a popular art' not only silly, but a little offensive. I do not claim to be able to judge poetry because I am a poet, though certainly the experience of trying to write verse is of great value to anyone trying to criticize poetry. But I claim some ability to judge poetry because it has been my profession to do just that for over twenty years now. In fitting myself to understand and to interpret literature I went through a training as long and arduous as your medical training. For you to set yourself up as a judge of my ability as a poetry editor and literary critic is about as silly as for me to begin criticizing your technique as a surgeon. I've no doubt some of your operations have not been entire successes, but I wouldn't jump to the conclusion that that was *your* fault; the patient might sometimes have been incurable, or in need of a blood transfusion that wasn't available. *De te, fabula.* Only a great deal of new blood, plus a skilled surgeon, will save CPM. I doubt if Mr. Bourinot is your man; if you saddle him too with Mr. O'Brien, then you might as well fold up now. You're going to have a lot more cancellations, and mine will be one of them.

> Cordially,
> Earle.

Marko's reply was a characteristically lighthearted apology, which soothed my feelings but could not alter our decision:

> Dear Earle,
> ... I'm a tycoon and have no real part in managing the magazine... We pay [O'Brien] $200 a year, and [the secretary] $100 [and] he gets about $300 worth of advertising. ... If we canned him we'd lose the advertising. Now, if I've got to fight with [him]... I quit. ... Why don't you write a snorter to the National Executive — it's their job but they too won't touch it!
>
> What you say about poetic judgement Earl is quite right. Joyce Marshall thinks the magazine has progressed wonderfully since you took over — it's just I'm behind the times & don't understand the oblique allusion, and such phrases as black light, or a white darkness etc. You do. And faith to me is not a fine flier. But then, they damned Keats. I'll never see much in Whitman except 'barbaric yawp'. De gustibus, etc.
>
> You may be right about Bourinot, but then who else is there? Pratt won't touch it.
>
> Affectionately,
> Marko.

I replied in part: "Thanks pal — I'm properly mollified. ... I'm going into a quiet corner and shriek with joy at no longer being an editor of anything."

It was another two months, however, before I could find that corner. First there was the polite farewell editorial to be written for the June issue. I said I made my living as a teacher and wanted to devote what little spare time I had to my own writing. "I cannot afford indefinitely the luxury of being an editor" (This was true, but I should have told myself all that two years earlier). I thanked my contributors who had associated themselves with me, "I could not have asked for more generous support than I have had from the outstanding poets and critics in this country." (Only true, of course, for those who shared my conception of "outstanding".) I confessed that the "difficulties of editing a magazine three thousand miles away from its business manager, circulation, secretary-treasurer, printer and publisher" had been wearying. I reminded our readers that CPM, like most poetry magazines, had never been self-supporting, though it was coming closer than ever to it in 1947: basic financing came from members or friends of the CAA. Poets in any authors' association, I said, "are inclined to

112

expect that the magazine will reflect their own poetic taste even if, as with the *Canadian Poetry Magazine*, such poets are a minority of the subscribers." I could not and wished not to fulfill such an expectation. The magazine's existence, for me, was justifiable "only by its becoming a genuinely contemporary organ with international standards and outlook." And so I thanked all who had helped, and wished Arthur Bourinot "all the luck in the world".

There were dozens of letters to answer from authors and editors across Canada, consoling me on the death of the new *CPM*. "Any file of the magazine," Floris McLaren, *CV*'s co-editor, wrote me, "will now have a record of what can be done even under CAA affiliation by a critically discriminating editor." In the east there was growing realization among writers of the threat to cultural standards posed by a bureaucratic organization whose President, once elected at an annual convention, could pick his own Board of Management which, in turn, picked both the editor of the poetry magazine and the chairman of the national literary awards board. And it was possible the CAA's president at this time, William Arthur Deacon, had been using his very considerable influence, as the well-known literary editor of the country's largest newspaper, to promote books of low quality but immediate "sales potential", at the expense of serious artists. If I had desired any further confirmation of this, after the Finch medal incident, it was given me in a letter which I was shown by a rebellious member of the B.C. executive of the CAA. Deacon had written her that he was now choosing the personnel of next year's Governor-General's Awards Committee, on which he said,"there would no longer be any professors. They don't know when a book is going to be popular." A tabloid-journalistic approach to literature.

By May, in Toronto and Montreal, some of my former *CPM* supporters — Sybil Hutchinson, Joyce Marshall, Pierre Berton, P.K. Page, and other writers and editors — were beginning to put together the nucleus of a rival organization to the CAA, tentatively called the Canadian Writers' Committee, and to consider developing a new national magazine to provide the sort of outlet for contemporary poetry and fiction which neither *CPM* nor the *Canadian Author and Bookman* would ever supply. Some thought we should unite to build one of the existing journals into national status. Alan Crawley, however, was steadfast in keeping his *Contemporary Verse* the small quarterly he could personally manage. *Northern Review* had apparently national aims, but quarrels among the editors had already caused the departure of most of them and reduced the magazine to a factional outlet for the somewhat juvenile John Sutherland, still finding a father-enemy in every older writer. Toronto's new magazine, *Here & Now*, alone seemed to offer possibilities.

I was at the moment weary of all organizations and longing to get away somewhere alone and start writing. But there were fifty copies of the Canadian number of *Outposts* to be sent out for review, and hundreds of exam papers to be marked, and gaps in the medieval section of the UBC library to be filled by thumbing through endless dealer-catalogues. There was our shack-home to be made shipshape for Roy Daniells and his bride to hide-out in for the summer. And before that Esther and Bill had to pack and be off for a summer in Europe, and the Lowrys party-ed away on a ship to the Caribbean.

By that time the June CPM was out and copies to be got onto stands. This number might have pacified some of the CAA's Old Guard if they hadn't now all been beyond parleying with, for the issue contained by coincidence a poem of Bourinot's and one by Audrey Alexandra Brown. On the other side, there was work by one of the *Northern Review* editors, Robert Simpson. To my mind the best poems in my final issue were all by women: Anne Hébert, P.K. Page, and Colleen Thibaudeau.

And then there was an article to write for the *Canadian Home Journal*.

1948

Yes, Canadians *Can* Read, But Do They?

(*Canadian Home Journal,* July 1948).

Nowadays the number of Canadians who cannot read or write in either the French or English language is satisfyingly small. But interviewing and testing several thousand Canadians during the recent war forced me to conclude that, though most of us know how to read, few of us do. And four years as literary editor of a Canadian monthly, plus two years as editor of a national poetry magazine, have taught me that although an almost unbelievable number of our citizens are secretly trying to create literary masterpieces very few have learned even the rudiments of self-expression in contemporary language. We are a literate country, yes; but for all the annual whoop-te-doos of the Canadian Authors' Association, the noisy backslapping that goes on in our book-review pages, the Governor-General's medals, and the multiplication of All-Canadian books, I wonder if we really are, even in 1948, a *literary* country.

Librarians (and newsstand proprietors) know better than I do what the average Canadian reads, but I am fairly certain of this, that most of our Joe Doakses with a grade school education (and some with a college degree) go happily through a calendar year without cracking a single hard-cover book. Joe is faithful only to the newspaper (headlines and first paragraphs of murder, rape and disaster stories; sports page; comics). If, in addition, he follows a magazine more or less regularly, five to one it's a cheap American "pulp".

And that of course is what's wrong with his reading and with the reading of most Canadians. It's an attempt to escape from life, rather than to get more out of it. It's not reading for pleasure, except to the extent that knocking oneself out is an effective way of avoiding having to think. Reading for pleasure, reading as a deliberately chosen and preferred entertainment and enrichment of living, is something that many a Canadian resorts to only if by some freak of circumstance he can't think of anything to work or play at, has no radio, movie, sport or other entertainment to turn to, no one to talk with, and no sleeping tablets handy. And it is our urban dwellers, because they have so many other distractions today, who read least of all — some of them only when flat on their backs in a hospital.

If you don't believe me, take a good look at the books you see next time you enter the "middle-class" home (income three to six thousand a year). Not counting the cookery manuals on the kitchen shelf, the obsolete "doctor's book" and the encyclopaedia father bought from a canvasser in the feckless Twenties — what have you? In terms of quantity, five to a hundred volumes. In terms of cash outlay, a little less than the cost of the bookcase, or one of the tires on the automobile in the garage. And a closer look will reveal that a good percentage are seedy heritages from childhood or from the last generation: Sunday School prizes, or faded Ralph Connors, Farnols, and Zane Greys that nobody in the house has looked at in years and never will again. The only reason they aren't sold to the secondhand store is that they would leave ugly gaps in the bookcase that aren't quickly filled by the occasional paperback Thorne Smith and bookclub best-sellers that constitute the present type of literary investment. There will of course be an imitation-leather trio — Shakespeare, the Bible, and Omar Khayyam (or, west of the Great Divide, Pauline Johnson) — wilting quietly in the embrace of a trick bookstand on the hall table. But you will hunt through many a substantial home before you find anything by a good Canadian novelist of the class of say Grove, Callaghan, MacLennan or Gweth Graham, or a living poet of any country. The classics? An odd Scott or Dickens with a bookmark at page twenty.

As for the libraries of our rich, they are, so far as the furtive and fitful observation of a professor can be any authority, often indistinguishable from those of the poor; occasionally extensive in a dull sort of way, sometimes even lush, but generally bearing few marks of use. Apart from my professional colleagues and arty friends, I have found the most lively interest in books to be among Canadians of low incomes living in remote places. The best and most-thumbed little library of poetry that I have seen in the last year was in the cabin of a West Coast fisherman who sees less cash in a month than some high-school students spend on corsages.

Such generalizations are probably even truer of Americans, but they are less true of the British or the continental European, despite shortages of paper and money. Europeans still get some of the kick out of reading that our grandparents did. And why don't we?

In the first place, we are the products of a school system which failed to convince us that reading was anything more than a duty. We learned to read so that we could carry, quite temporarily, a burden of facts; and we learned to write so that we could deposit that burden, at a set time, on an examination paper and forget it. We were given that approach not only to factual subjects like chemistry or history but to literature. Until I got to university I read poetry mainly when told to and sometimes in a wall-eyed fashion — one optic alert for the all-important footnotes, and the other photographing the required "memory passages". And if I hadn't been lucky in my professors, I might have gone through university without discovering the mysterious and profound pleasures of simply "playing" a great poem to one's self as if it were music, or finding that enlargement of understanding about oneself and one's fellow beings that can come from the unhurried, unexamined, unrequired "soaking in" of a well-wrought novel.

I'm told that all these evils have been eliminated by the modern schools, and I know that some of them have. But at least eighty per cent of my freshmen students arrived in my class convinced that poetry was a mug's game, reading-for-pleasure an occupation for aged invalids, and literature courses a waste of time for a man who has to make his way in this world. Nor do I flatter myself that I have seriously reduced the percentage.

For the teacher, from grade school to university, is up against a System. He has to teach, for the purpose of an examination, what his superiors have decided are the proper texts, and his superiors have too often been unable to tell a good text from a bad, or had to choose among several bad ones. I am well aware that compilers of school anthologies, as well as choosers of them, are genuine educational specialists. But I have met too many of them who are ignorant of the literature of our times, cursed with puritanical inhibitions, and unwilling to recall what they themselves read with pleasure when they were adolescents. Much of what is still served up as modern Canadian poetry to our high school students is only the late barren blossoming of minor Victorian Sarah Binkses. . . .

Adolescents want adventurous literature but they don't want kid-stuff; they burn to project themselves into the adult world they see about them and if they aren't given a chance to do it through good literature they will do it through bad, through the cheapest kind of pulp thriller to be picked up at the corner drug store. And they will prefer this sort of fare, which at first glance seems nearer to their real (or Kinsey) life, to books that have been rendered psychologically false in the interests of an outmoded morality to which even their parents are paying not much more than lip-service. Nor can you stimulate them by dull, politically "safe" fiction which shrinks from the realities of an atom-bomb civilization. I honestly believe that a bolder and more adult selection of reading in our high schools would be reflected in decreased buying of sex-and-killer magazines, and, consequently, in a decrease of juvenile delinquency.

Secondly, quite apart from the inhibitions imposed by our educational system, our literary maturity is held back by the plain lack of good books in this country, outside the big cities. As one of Canada's outstanding librarians remarked to me recently, you can't expect people to raise their literary taste if they haven't anything to raise it on. Far too many of our citizens are without the facilities of public libraries and, with the mounting cost of books and journals, without the money to create their own.

117

Of those who can afford to buy, too few are told what is worth buying, either by librarians, book reviewers, or radio critics. Book reviewing has been improving in quality but it still too often represents the hasty and perhaps untutored judgment of an overworked newspaperman. In particular, very few critics are trying to tell us what are the best books of *other* countries; few, except the young intellectual in the obscure "little-mag", are striving to keep us in touch with world literature and world thought today, so that we may have a standard by which to judge ourselves and to grow in stature.

This ignorance of genuinely contemporary literature, an ignorance which constitutes a distinct cultural difference between a literary-minded citizen of Toronto and one, say of London, New York or Paris, in turn handicaps our coming writers. Hundreds and hundreds of people with literary talent in this country never write a thing worth printing because they scarcely ever read anything of their own times that is worth reading, and their idiom continues to betray the colonial time-lag, the poetic diction or fruity prose of a hundred years ago. I am not suggesting that the Canadian need be an imitator of foreign writers, of Hemingway or Kafka, Auden or Dylan Thomas. But I am suggesting that if he has no acquaintance with them he is making it a lot harder for himself to speak in the accents of a modern man.

Mind you, if a Canadian does write a thoroughly contemporary novel, original in treatment, significant in theme, international in outlook, he may get it published in Canada or he may not. Publishers are in the business to make money, and most of them print the books they feel sure Canadians will buy, not what they may suspect it would be most maturing for this nation to read.

While we're at it, let's take a smack at magazine editors too. Though I think there has been a considerable general improvement in the quality of our more popular magazines lately, there are still Canadian editors who will reject the unknown poet until he gets a book out and wins a medal, and hold aloof from the new fiction writer until he makes a sale across the border — and even then "come a-courtin' too slow."

And yet perhaps the most unreliable people in this country to consult about literary matters are the writers themselves. There are some real authors, both in the ranks and in the leadership of the Canadian Authors' Association, Canadians who are genuinely trying to be literary artists and to interpret themselves and this country honestly, regardless of whether they sell a book; but such folk are a small percentage of the nine-hundred-odd self-confessed scribes, and the prestige of the few is exploited by the Philistinism of the many. By and large, it seems to me that the Canadian Authors' Association has encouraged the notion that any novel is worth buying if it has a Canadian setting and observes all the tabus of the Manse, and that the best authors are those who make the most money in the least time; on the other hand, the young experimentalist, or anyone in revolt against literary jingoism and antimacassar motto-writing, is too often attacked (or worse, ignored) for the qualities which may make him an important builder of our culture: literary honesty, technical originality, moral courage.

There is, of course, no quick solution to the problem of Canadian puritanism and parish-pumpery, any more than to the general international utilitarianism of our age, all of which impede Canadians from climbing past the literate to the literary level. We live in a world where art must compete with the artificial, the poems of Eliot with syndicated doggerel, and where, moreover, the buyers are uneducated to the difference and the makers are corrupted with the belief that the quality of their product is decided by the price it fetches.

This is not Renaissance Italy. By and large it is much easier to find money to support a local hockey team than either a symphony, an art gallery or a literary magazine. Nor is this Soviet Russia, where the State makes millionaires out of its artists, so long as they glorify the State — and drives them to artistic or physical suicide when they step out of line. Our sins are democratic, the sins of omission.

Yet just because we live in a democracy, genuine though imperfect, every one of us can do something towards raising our literary standards. It is because I live in Vancouver and not Leningrad that I can publish here my belief (which may not be at all shared by the editors of this magazine or by Ottawa) that our federal governments, past and present, have been dilatory and penny-pinching and unimaginative in their support of literature. If enough people join me in expressing that belief and in agitating for such immediate and practical items as annual Dominion bursaries for young writers, such reforms will be brought about.

If, on the other hand, you believe that the arts thrive better from private support, and enough of you make a noise about that, you will undoubtedly shame some of our wealthy ones into more generous acts of patronage. In time, perhaps, you can teach them, too, that the act of donating money to an art does not in itself make one a judge of that art.

Even if you don't believe in direct financial aid to writers, you can help to raise literary standards simply by writing and telling the author, the editor or the publisher when you have read something worth reading (as well as when you haven't), and by buying the book or subscribing to the journal (or, if you honestly can't afford it, by seeing that your library does). If you are a teacher you can try, as many do, to make literature an adventure toward adulthood rather than an infantile chore; if you are a parent you can wake up your parent-teacher association to campaign for honest and contemporary texts. And every voter bears the responsibility for the continuance of horse-

and-buggy Ministries of Education, and the absence of good rural library systems.

Finally, if you're mad and tormented enough to want to be a writer, and so contribute directly to our literature, then there is nothing for it but to be yourself. Don't worry whether you are writing like a Canadian (or as a Canadian, or American, publisher would like you to write). Set down what you know best and what has moved you most deeply; shape it with all the living craft you can summon, and whatever is peculiar about being a Canadian will surely begin to glow somewhere in your words. But for Apollo's sake, stop being provincial; be aware of your country as a whole and as a small but symbolic part of the round world today. Don't worry about sprouting maples; get your taproot down under the gravel in your own backyard, and hike those branches up into the international air and the interstellar sun. Then Canada will begin at last to take its place among the literary nations.

As I Remember

The Lowrys had left me the key to their Dollarton shack, to use for the summer. I had my bag packed, with notes for writing *Turvey*, when the mounting floods in the Fraser River valley reached disaster heights. The navy took over and called for volunteers. I joined, and spent the next ten days "captaining" a power-boat on anti-looting patrol. Coming from that adventure to the utter quietness of Lowry's squatter-shack was too much of a switch. I moved again, to my friend Einar's Bowen Island retreat. There the conditions were ideal. Einar worked in the city all week while his Alsatian and the brindle cat and I took care of Lieben, the cliff house, and wrote *Turvey*. On the weekends there were visitors willing to listen while I tried out the latest chapter.

Occasionally I'd row down to the Cove for mail. It was good to hear, through Sergeant, of the reactions to the Canadian number of his *Outposts*. CPM's poets, said the British, have more vitality and originality. I wondered if they would maintain that opinion for long.

In Canada there was very little reaction to the issue. This was partly because O'Brien, unknown to me, had failed to send out a single review copy and had even refused to fill orders for copies. This I learned later from Gustafson; he had contributed to the issue and then sent a cheque for three extra copies; his order was returned with rude marginalia in O'Brien's hand. I had to obtain extra copies from England and mail them out belatedly from Vancouver. With each I included a letter pointing out this was the first time a London literary magazine had brought out a Canadian issue.

One of the critics I wrote to was E.K. Brown; I asked him if he would mention the special number in his annual survey of Canadian literature. He thanked me for the copy, "which contains so many very good things. I might have missed a lot of pleasure. I hope the English are at least interested," It was Brown, however, who proved not sufficiently interested even to list the issue when he came to write his survey. The Canadian issue of London *Outposts*, a 2-year project, became a non-event in Canada. In Britain it was favourably reviewed by the *Times* and a half-dozen other journals.

In the mail there were also some fascinating reports from my eastern friends of the CAA's 1948 conference in Ottawa. The lady with the black tights was there, reciting the poems of Joy Tranter, chairperson of the Management Committee, who in turn was conducting a Verse Round Table for new members. There was a post-mortem session on the CPM, presided over by none other than John Murray Gibbon. He called upon Mrs. Tranter to speak, introducing her with the remark that he knew her well because they went to the same Turkish baths. He went to reduce, he said, but one could see at a glance that Mrs. Tranter had no need to take baths on that score, so he assumed that she took them because, for the last two years, she had suffered a pain in the neck from reading the *Canadian Poetry Magazine*. He was glad that the magazine was once more emerging from the bearded state. And so on. Leslie Barnard made a polite speech in defense of the need of the young to be different — no names mentioned. Bourinot then announced that the new policy ot CPM would be "traditional but with a reasonable amount of experimentation". He would not say what sort of experiments.

Just before I returned to UBC in September I got my last missive from the immortal O'Brien. It was demanding a financial settlement from me in closing out the Vancouver office of CPM: $33.07 for subscriptions and stamp money. This was the precise figure, in fact, which I had long ago reported to him and paid him. Since O'Brien's letter indicated a copy of it had gone to Mrs. Whyte, the CAA's secretary, I sent her at once a photocopy of my cancelled cheque with O'Brien's signature on the back. Neither of them favoured me with a reply, but I later learned that within a week of my letter O'Brien was finally fired. He was replaced as Business Manager by Mrs. Whyte.

The September CPM listed me as joint editor, presumably because some of it Bourinot had inherited from me. He had not, however, sent me proofs, and I continued for some months to get angry letters from poets whose work had been accepted but not printed, or misprinted and not paid for.

I broke my seclusion at Lieben only once, going into town to take part in a radio panel.

How Can We Raise Canada's Cultural Standards?
Radio broadcast, "Town Meeting in Canada", Vancouver, 1948

To begin with, let's try to be clear about this word "culture". Do we mean what Matthew Arnold meant by the term: "a knowledge of the best that has been thought and said in the world?" To me culture means that and more. It begins in a nation when its people not only know the best of other people's art but are creating their own. You can have too much of Matthew Arnold's culture; Victoria, B.C. had too much of it when its art critics and art buyers were so busy looking at reproductions of Landseer and Corot they didn't notice Emily Carr until she was dead, couldn't see her woods for Corot's trees.

The same thing continues to happen in every Canadian city when a creator appears in its midst. The artist is neglected, starved out into making ads or jingles or carving kitsch or teaching or tap-dancing or some other commercialization of his talents, partly because he hasn't yet been noticed by the very people who should be sponsoring him. The "cultured" Canadians are too bemused with their gift copies of the latest illustrated-history-of-ancient-art-in-one-volume, or the American Book-of-the-Month, or deafened by this year's perfect recordings of the Brandenburg concertos.

It's true, of course, that Canada needs lots more subsidized libraries, art galleries, ballet companies and symphonies if it is really to cut a figure in the world. To raise the cultural level of our smaller towns we will have to find a way to support a few string quartets as well as three hundred thousand juke-boxes; an amateur theatre in each town as well as forty movie-cathedrals; and an art gallery for every thousand pulp-magazine stands.

But all of this is just so much sleep-walking unless we are finding a way also to encourage our young composers, painters, poets, our creative as well as our performing artists.

Detection of talent, to begin with. Our system, or lack of system, of scholarships in this country puts a premium on the potential scientist and the academic swot; we need more contests and rewards to discover the possible actor or dancer or sculptor or dramatist in every school and to send him on for training in the basic crafts of his art. Then, when the artist begins producing, we, his audience, ought to make sure that he can put us in touch with his work. We are supposed to have some fairly good painters in Canada. How many smalltowners ever get a chance to see a travelling exhibit of their work, or of anybody's work?

123

In my Creative Writing classes at U.B.C. in the last two years, I have found at least a dozen students with positive literary ability. I have a growing stack of their short stories. One or two have been published, but most haven't been and probably won't be published except on this campus, though they are better, culturally better, stories than what the big Canadian "slicks" print every month. They are rejected because they are experimental in form, or too honest in language or unorthodox in sentiment. We need magazines and book firms in this country that don't have to please big advertising corporations and the lowest level of public taste. The only answer is to subsidize the printing of good literature.

In fact nearly all my suggestions involve money. Jacques Singer* knows it would take money to create symphony orchestras, Bert Binning knows it would take money to multiply art galleries, Gordon Hilker knows it takes lots of money to put on the best dramas and concerts, whether home-grown or from outside. The argument should be — not, do we need money? but, how do we get it?

Well, you can only get money from whoever has it. And you get it by asking them for it or taxing it out of them. I don't care too much which way it's got; but I suggest that taxation can provide a surer income for planning cultural development than private charities, which put artist and performer at the mercy of his patron's whims, and wouldn't, in Canada, provide enough even then. Of course government patronage puts the artist at the mercy of governmental whims, but I'll take my chance with freely-elected governments. However, until we who work in arts find the way to persuade our representatives to greatly increase the outlays for cultural development, our arts will continue to be starved and our cultural standards will not rise but sink.

---

*Singer, at that time conductor of the Vancouver Symphony, and the late B.C. Binning, painter, and Hilker, impresario, were the other members of the panel for this "Town Meeting".

As I Remember

1948 (October) - 1949 (February)

That summer of '48, while I was on Bowen, Authors Anonymous had proved itself an adult organization, surviving happily without its founder. Harlow, Jackson and Paul Wright read fresh writing at it, until they left in September to take up their graduate fellowships in the Iowa Creative Writing School. Bill and Alice McConnell brought AA their fiction and there were some important recruits. One was George Robertson, a brilliant sophomore already writing mature short stories, but being required, by UBC's academic straightjacket, to wait two years before he could enrol in my workshop. (George is now one of the CBC's leading television producers). Another was Eric Nicol, filling a witty column for a downtown paper that summer before sailing for France and graduate studies at the Sorbonne. I had known and admired him since his undergraduate days when, as "Jabez", he became the funniest columnist the *Ubyssey* had ever had. There was even a plaque up in the Student Union building to commemorate his graduation. Now he was writing plays, and anxious to have the benefit of AA criticisms.

When the UBC fall term began, however, the graduates departed and there were only five "actives" left, all undergraduate bachelors with no place to entertain each other. The sad but logical solution was faced: AA stopped being anonymous, named its five legitimate members and its half-dozen grad "associates" and its "honorary member", Prof. Birney, and was granted the status of a campus club, with a slice of the Alma Mater Society's budget and the right to meet in campus chambers.

My three writer-fellows in Iowa wrote me at length. They were all teaching "bonehead English" (to Jackson's chagrin, he being one of our first-class honour grads in English), and none of them was happy about the guidance they were getting in their writing — "motivated by self-interest and geared to commercialism", wrote Jackson. One professor was on a commission basis with a New York magazine and coaching his students to write for it. Both Jackson and Wright complained of an atmosphere of backbiting, gossip, spite between the instructors. It sounded to me remarkably like the English department back in Vancouver, but I couldn't tell them so. Harlow, however, was about to marry and perhaps stay forever.

Meanwhile Eric Nicol was writing me from the Sorbonne that its doctorate was "something awarded to the mentally retarded foreigner", worthless to his own career whether that was to be writing or teaching. He had arrived at "the almost painful conviction that we have all we need for writing in our own back yard, and a fine fresh breeze that comes from where people aren't".

There was again a great rush of applicants for the Creative Writing class, and some very promising writing submitted in advance. Among those I chose were two already-established women journalists, Jean Howarth and Evelyn Caldwell.

I found it still necessary to beg the university library to buy contemporary poets. In my October day-book there is a long list of authors still unavailable to UBC students, including such Europeans as Graham Greene, Kafka, Maritain, O'Flaherty, Silone, Spender, Stephen Zweig; and Americans of the stature of Aiken, Fearing, Henry Miller, Ransom, Rexroth, Shapiro, Stevens, Tate and Warren. With such gaps in the library of British Columbia's only university, it was difficult to provoke much attention for the absence also of poetry by mere Canadians. UBC did not as yet possess a book by Gustafson or Klein.

Robertson Davies, whom I had not yet met, had written me in July that he had read my *Canadian Home Journal* article in his doctor's office and was warmly in agreement with it. Even many of the Canadians who do read, he felt, "are incapable of holding their culture like gentlemen". He was particularly appreciative of my remarks about the CAA, which he had declined to join because it manifested the faults of the worst trade unions in that it "protects incompetent craftsmen". I replied that I valued very much the opinions of the author of the *Diary of Samuel Marchbanks*. For me, the greatest evil created by the CAA was that it pretended to represent the living authors of Canada, and because it tolerated only childish or cheap writing, it made Canadian literary culture appear ridiculous in the eyes of outsiders. What was probably needed was a rival organization with higher standards, though at the moment I wanted not to be organized at all. Davies replied at once that he agreed and was willing to join me in working for such an organization, whose members would be carefully selected.

I answered that his letters had encouraged me to break completely with the CAA, and I attached a copy of my resignation. I sent the letter to Philip Child, the Bursar of the CAA, because I thought him to be a man whose fiction showed craftsmanship and sensitivity. When he did not reply I published it in *Here & Now*. Eventually Child wrote *Saturday Night* a letter which revealed he was perhaps still ignorant of the sabotage that some other members of the CAA had carried out against my editorship, and content in any case to accept the poetic standards set by the Gibbons and the O'Briens.

Extracts from my letter to Child follow, and from a summation of my experience with CPM which was somewhat belatedly invited from me by the CAA's house organ, the *Canadian Author and Bookman*, fourteen years later.

126

"Age Shall Not Wither Thee"

Letter to Philip Child dated 15 November 1948; published in *Here &
Now*, Toronto, January 1949.

I joined the CAA in 1946 after considerable hesitation, arising from
several years of reading the official organs and hearing the official
speeches of leading members of the Association. These had led me to
feel that the CAA was primarily concerned with boosting the literary
products of its members, whether they be good or bad, and not
infrequently also in leading the attack on the healthy attempts at experimentation among younger writers. Nevertheless I felt that I could not
in fairness judge the Association without becoming one of its members
and working within it for a more liberal approach to literary art. Since
that time until I resigned from the editorship of the *Canadian Poetry
Magazine* in June of this year I have worked to the best of my ability,
and often to the detriment of my own writing, to promote the point of
view that I held, both by participation in the work of local branches
and by editing the *Canadian Poetry Magazine*. I have now come to
realize that the attitude of the majority of the Association, or at least of
the members who control its public statements, makes further participation on my part both a waste of time and a compromise of my artistic
principles.

. . . In the CAA a writer's success is judged by his sales, his ability to
win local prizes or to say kind things about his own wares and the
wares of the leading figures in the Association. The standards of judgment are those of the Victorian age only. . .   . . . The CAA, to my
mind, is predominantly a body of aging hacks and reactionaries who
maintain a dubious prestige simply by persuading a number of
genuine writers such as yourself to represent them in the public eye. It
is for this reason particularly that I have come to feel the CAA is actually
a hindrance to the growth of a mature literary culture in this country. It
compromises the serious artist by associating him with its attacks on
the younger writer's experimentalism and with its general puritanical
and venal approach to the problem of writing. I think the time has
come for the serious writer in this country to break with the CAA and
form a guild of craftsmen who stand for the principles of artistic freedom and integrity and sound standards of craftsmanship. I can only
hope that you yourself will come to agree with me. To age is common,
but not as the CAA ages, for by its hostility to the work of the young it
fails to renew itself with the blood of youth.

Canadian Poetry Magazine **1946-48**

Retrospective article, *Canadian Author & Bookman*, Winter 1963.

When I took over CPM in 1946 I hoped to turn it into a reasonably professional journal with at least a national, as distinct from parochial, coverage and with standards high enough to get attention and approval internationally from the contemporary-minded. I chose my editorial associates from members of the staff at the University of British Columbia who shared my aims. After two years we all resigned. What happened?

The trouble was that we succeeded. We took over a magazine which was publishing almost exclusively the work of a small group writing in a sort of colonial Georgian; by our eighth and last issue we were publishing virtually all the good younger Canadian poets (who had up to then ignored or been ignored by CPM): Klein, Page, Smith, Anderson, Dudek, Souster, Livesay, Gustafson, Miriam Waddington, Finch, Marriott, Bailey, Hambleton, McLaren, Bruce, Kay Smith, Simone Routier, Wreford. I don't think anyone could argue now that these weren't leading Canadian poets of the Forties, and their support gave me the kind of assurance I needed at the time; but today I'm equally glad that, in our efforts to win them, we didn't miss too many of the little-knowns who were to come into prominence in the next decade, such as Anne Wilkinson, Daniells, Whalley, Anne Hébert, Cogswell. These we published, as well as three whose work and reputations were not to be fully appreciated till the Sixties: James Reaney, Al Purdy and the late Malcolm Lowry. I wish we could claim to have printed also, by 1948, Avison and Layton (at least we didn't turn them down) and to have secured more Canadian poetry in the French language. We published some, anyway, and I think we were the first English-Canadian magazine ever to do so.

Among the other "firsts" were the earlier version of Pratt's "Behind the Log", two translations from the Eskimo; and an entire issue given over to British poetry of the day, selected by Howard Sergeant, editor of the London *Outposts*. At the same time I prepared a Canadian number of his journal — an international exchange which resulted not only in the sly smuggling of fresh Canadian poetry into London but in the appearance first in Canada of new poems by such well-known poets as Treece and Heath-Stubbs, and by others who have since moved to the foreground: Comfort, Muriel Spark, Kirkup, Abse, and Denise Levertov. Given another year we would probably have found a kindred American journal to swap an issue with; I was working on this when we resigned.

Within Canada itself we managed to find poems from every province and from poets whose years ran from eighty-six (Duncan Campbell Scott) down to eighteen. About forty percent of our contributors were under thirty. I can see now, of course, that there were times when my eagerness to print somebody young from somewhere new somewhat befogged my critical judgments.

Still, as I riffle those old pages, I come across things I'm glad we gave light to. They move me, as I re-read them now, as strongly as they did when they popped out of the mail. An editor has little else to go by, for reassurance in after years.

CPM was costing only a little more than a thousand dollars a year to publish; it was possible, in a good quarter, to bring in $250 in advertising for an issue. With a little effort, small donors or "life subscribers" could be found to fetch us out of the red — at first. The regular subscribers' list, which had been down to a few hundred when we took over, began to move toward the thousand mark, and we acquired in particular a number of solid U.S. university library subscriptions, which incline to be permanent once undertaken. However, new subscriptions did not help; in fact they were liabilities; the magazine still sold for two dollars a year, a price fixed a decade before, in the Depression. And the Business Manager would not change it. Nor could I overrule him; not only was he (and the entire "management" staff of the magazine) three thousand miles away in Toronto, he was also not under my control at all, but in theory at least under that of the Canadian Authors' Association, the owners. In practice he went his own way. Since he was an octogenarian in failing health and faculties, who disliked any poetry later than Sir Walter Scott's, his way was not our way. Those in his office who were loyal to the editors were quickly forced into resignation and replaced by incompetents loyal to him and the Old Guard in poetry. He openly complained about the content being illogical "rubbish", and deliberately put obstacles in the way of publishing it. He found even Pratt's *Behind the Log* too "modern" and incomprehensible to merit publication. He was, of course, entitled to his opinion. It was an honest one and he was a well-meaning man — in the wrong job.

All this would have been easily resolved if the owners had replaced him with a competent younger person, or had even been willing to keep the magazine solvent by subsidies, as had been promised. Instead, the business manager was allowed to become the rallying garrison for those versifiers in the CAA whom James Reaney later described as, at the best, "metrical smoothies without a metaphor to their bones", and otherwise simple "metrical hobblers". Specialists in local poetry competitions, and in Edgar Guestian doggerel for rural newspapers, mountainous or emaciated suburban socialites with three names and a thousand Victorian prejudices, they approved of nothing written since Rupert Brooke, and not always of him. They organized a systematic cancellation of subscriptions of CPM within the CAA; they sent a steady stream of letters of complaint to CAA against the editors; they threatened that organization with their withdrawal unless we opened our pages to them and excluded the "moderns". There were others in the CAA, of course, perhaps the majority, who were on the side of our kind of CPM, but they were not as well organized. When the inefficiency and hostility in the Toronto managerial office began to involve even the bookkeeping and the payment of certain contributors, I found the situation too exhausting in mind and spirit, and too compromising. My staff resigned with me.

It's painful to open old wounds — but it can sometimes help the patient. CPM is once again trying to recover from anaemic decline. I hope that this time the editor will have the loyalty of his financial backers, and that whoever they are they won't be buffaloed by a few life-hating ancients.

Mr. Pepys Listens to CBC Radio

"Critically Speaking", CBC Trans-Canada, November 14, 1948.

November seventh. The *Lord's* Day, and fine brave sunshine as may not come again for many a Sunday. So my wife and I into the car and along the North Shore to sniff the sea and walk in woods. Back betimes, tuning into NBC and its *Album of Familiar Music* (which doth grow too familiar each week to my taste) and anon in my favourite chair for *Stage 49.*

But it proved not all to our fancy. Though Master Hugh MacLennan I do heartily admire, for there is none doth write a better novel in our land these days, yet this latest of his, that all do talk of, *The Precipice,* do seem to me to walk astray somehow from the subject it did intend. God knows we in Canada are plagued and bullied enough by Puritans still, so that the writing about them should make a most shrewd entertainment; and by compare with Americans we lack enterprise and do hide our lights under a monstrous bushel of simpering. Yet for the life of me I could not but think my wife's thumb at fault and she tuned to a soap opera. For here was the beauteous heroine suffering beyond all belief from her flinthearted sisters, and most perversely dealt with by her lover. And he a great booby, surely, and no sophisticated man of New York, who would fail to acquaint his affianced with the news that his spouse was at pains to divorce him, or indeed with the intelligence that he did have a spouse at all. I do confess that Master MacLennan's new book I have yet to read, and reflect that it may be but the cruelty of radio which hath squeezed his fable till it do seem like nothing more than the tale of the innocent country maiden who doth with no great credence at last reform the city rake, and he surely but a Toronto broker in disguise.

But I do confess that we were attentive to the end and did switch off Ozzie and Harriet that we might fall to talking about Stephen Lassiter and Lucy Cameron — which is what Master MacLennan would have us do, and our thanks to him. But mighty careful we were to switch on again for the most admirable fresh talking of Masters Gilmour and Sinclair. I do not know which to admire the more, Master Clyde for the pith and forthrightness of his wit, or Master Lister for the pregnancy and moving passion of his speech. And certainly I do revel in their brains and the blessed clarity of their speaking, and pray mightily that our governors reward them that they be not lured from us, like Lucy Cameron, to the fleshpots of the South.

Pleased that my wife judges them so too, for she doth read and see

131

more than I — though in secret a little vexed she should sigh so prettily over Master Gilmour, and fall to lamenting even that he was never let to play the whole of his mincing music cue.

And so to *Classics for Today*, from Vancouver Town, which I be told cannot be heard by our eastern citizens, more's the pity. Monsieur de Rimminocz and his strings did delight our ear with Peter Warlock his *Capriol Suite*, and gave us strength to attend the ten o'clock news and meditate on the affairs of state that grow more grievous each day, for all the cool and serene tone which it is the custom now to use in announcing the most alarming of bulletins. And so to bed.

Monday, the eighth. Much business this day and time only to hear the merry new farce of Master Eric Nicol, the Stag at Eve, from the Vancouver Theatre. I do think Master Nicol to be as fertile and sprightly a wit as our radio gives us, if sometime his pace be more for the eye than the ear. And I did lament that his tale of the little man who wins love by his jests were not heard across the land, for Producer MacDonald offered it happily, Master Bernard Braden graced it with his acting, and Master John Avison married it to a most engaging raillery of music.

Tuesday, the ninth. Full of busyness again and much vexed that affairs held me beyond the first half of Master Robert Allens' *Heritage of Music*. But I did hear the charming strains of our good Doctor Gagnier, which Master Avison and his *Concert Orchestra* fell to playing, to my simple ears, as delectably as could be wished.

Wednesday, the tenth. Mightily vexed at my wife that she did choose this night to be home to a great gathering of females, but recovered my spirits finding she had contrived with Captain Cuttle I should take supper at his lodgings, for he and his lady be excellent company and most skilled in matters of radio, and she merry to look upon and a great cook.

But I do think I took little ease in the prodigious long recitations from the nineteenth century that came first to our ears. I could have wished my friend, the good Doctor Bissell, had given us pieces more pithy and from a greater diversity of authors, and some that were lively as well as profound. And I could wish as well that his readers, fine actors though they be, would speak less like curates from pulpits when they come to grapple with verse.

But we grew content again with the new musique of Master Harry Somers that was a continual fresh rain on the mind. As for Master Bernard Trotter and his ingenious play of the world in 1848, that he calleth *Portrait of a Year*, I did find it as lively and profitable a lesson in history as ever I did hear. And all bodied forth with that skill in acting and dexterity in presentation which do make the name of Master

Andrew Allan justly famed over all our continent.

And so to the Opera Bouffet of *The Telephone*, and still pretty merry though not so perfectly so, though the music full of mirth and satire — for musicians did too assiduously come between us and the words. And Captain Cuttle, my host, did remark the piece to have fared better when he saw it on the stage in New York, where the miming of the actors could rescue it from the dreariness of making the same jest too many a time.

And so, after much good converse with mine hosts, to home, where my wife, poor drudge, was washing great quantities of platters after her party.

Thursday, the eleventh. Up betimes and mightily occupied with an *Armistice Day Program* to make use of some of my own scribbles for the Dominion Network. And Lord! I did watch with delight but no little embarrassment how producer Robert Allen, the actors, engineers, and Master Avison and his musicians, must come mightily to the rescue of my poor words. And so home, musing on the infinite shifts of man, and his desire always for delight and content, and yet his will to kill his fellows in pursuit of that desire. But greatly pleased to find Master Read and his wife for company, and a tender enough chicken, which we afford seldom enough these days, but the Lord be thanked my wife did purchase this week without departing out of her allowance.

Friday the twelfth. For the first time contrived that I should listen to the *Canadian Short Story Program* but did find, as I feared, fifteen minutes to be but scurvy space for the telling of a good tale, for a tale doth need flesh and blood more than any wile of plot, or whistling of wind in the trees. And I did resolve to write the Governors of the CBC praying that they would find the half of an hour each day for our tale-tellers.

Anon the *Citizens Forum* and my wife in great content until the Master of Cermonies did call upon a lady in his company to give us the *Viewpoint on Town Planning.* And ever since my wife doth plague me to make protest, saying it do cast a condescension on her sex to think it should have any peculiar opinion about the Planning of Towns, that there be only one opinion about such matters in our land, to wit that there *is* no Planning, but should be, and any man would say the same. But I could make nothing of her argument. And so to bed.

Saturday, the thirteenth. And much to hear no doubt, but I all day bedevilled with a rheum in the head and miserable with my diary, which do read this week as wretchedly as if some college tutor had been at the writing of it.

133

1949

Why Is Canada Still Banning Joyce's *Ulysses*?
CBC Radio Talk, 9 March 1949.

A few days ago I was looking through the latest issue of that intelligent new Toronto magazine, *Here and Now*, and came across a long article by the noted Montreal poet, Abraham Klein, from a book which he's preparing, a new interpretation of James Joyce's novel, *Ulysses*. It's one of the curious contradictions of Canada's literary life that a respectable Montreal lawyer would want to write, and a respectable Toronto journal would publish, a commentary on a novel which the Government of Canada still forbids to be imported. Moreover it's possible, and has been for many years, to buy in Canadian bookshops any of the dozen or so books of criticism and analysis which distinguished American and British critics have written about James Joyce's most famous work. You can even purchase in Canadian bookstores a large hunk of *Ulysses* in the Viking Press's *Portable James Joyce*. But if you were to drive south of the border and buy *Ulysses* itself (as you can without difficulty, since it's legal in the United States, and widely distributed in a Modern Library edition), and try to bring it home, you'd have the book seized and destroyed at the border, and you would be liable to a fine and even the confiscation of your automobile.

What sort of a book is this which is treated like cocaine or infected fruit by the Canadian Customs and is just regulation book-fare for Americans and most Europeans? Or, a better question, what sort of a country is this Canada of ours where it's possible for a six-year-old to walk into a store and buy lurid and highly uncomic comic-books illustrating the scientific way to strangle another child if he doesn't like him, and adolescents to acquire magazines glamourizing the lives of contemporary swindlers and murderers, but forbids the import and sale of the most influential single novel of the twentieth century?

I admit I feel strongly on this subject, for it's not one classic or even one greater author we persecute. There is in fact a continuous and indiscriminate banning of serious works of literary art being perpetrated in this country. It is being done by minor bureaucrats without literary cause or literary judgment. Here are some of the books which (according to a recent "secret" governmental list supplied only to booksellers) cannot be imported into Canada:

No. 1: James T. Farrell's *Bernard Clare,* the latest novel by one of America's most respected and serious writers. I've read this book: it is authentic art, realistic in technique, deeply moral in its sociological implications. In no way is it "pornographic, seditious or obscene", to use the terms operative in our Customs Act.

No. 2: the complete translation by Sir Richard Burton of the *Arabian Nights,* which is the most scholarly version known, and the most readable.

No. 3: several volumes of the short stories of Guy de Maupassant.

No. 4: the famous *Droll Stories* of another major French writer, Balzac.

No. 5: The Journal of Albion Moonlight, a poetic and intellectual work by the distinguished American poet, Kenneth Patchen.

And so on, and so on: books by D.H. Lawrence, Leon Trotsky, Emma Goldman, Frank Harris, Francois Mauriac, Colette, Erskine Caldwell, Marie Stopes, Victor Marguerite, Ben Hecht, Remy de Gourmont, Irving Stone, William Faulkner *(Sanctuary),* Radcliffe Hall, Maxwell Bodenheim, Margaret Sanger — all authentic works of art or science. They circulate freely in the U.S. and in most of the English-speaking world, yet they are forbidden the eyes of Canadians, and lumped in one list with the cheapest sort of sexy paper-backs turned out by the specialists in pornographic hackwriting. And of all of these works muzzled by the great woolly muffler of the Dominion's Department of Customs and Excise, none seems to me to be in more urgent need of unmuzzling than James Joyce's *Ulysses.*

So curious are the contradictions of our literary scene that I apparently risk my legal neck even by trying to talk about such a wicked work. In fact at one time today it looked as if this broadcast tonight might be cancelled because, though opinion was that I could *talk* about a banned book, I couldn't *quote* from one. Fortunately, however, the quotations which I had selected turn out to be included in the Kosher selections from *Ulysses* in the *Portable James Joyce* I mentioned earlier, or in the Anderson and Walton's *This Generation* — another anthology of modern literature which circulates legally in Canada. This means that I'll be able to quote without the entire CBC being jailed, and me.

As far back as 1938, when the University of Toronto, my employer at that time, asked me to give a public lecture in Toronto on James Joyce, I wrote the Collector of Customs and Excise in the National Revenue Division of the Dominion Government, Ottawa (who, curiously enough, is still our sole censor in these matters) asking how I could get hold of *Ulysses* in order to lecture, whether it could be reprinted in Canada and whether, supposing I already had a copy, was I liable to arrest for quoting publicly from it? The Collector of Customs wrote me the following reply — "*Ulysses* by James Joyce has been prohibited importation into Canada since January 1923. No exception is made in the case of individuals. As to whether or not it is illegal for a Canadian publisher to re-print this book and if it is illegal to possess a copy of the book in Canada, these are questions which do not refer to matters coming under the jurisdiction of this Department. It is possible that you may be able to obtain some information from your Chief of Police in regard thereto. Yours truly, etc." That ominous last sentence I've puzzled over from time to time during the last eleven years but it hasn't somehow deterred *me* from reading the whole of *Ulysses* — I daren't say how — or from lecturing about it and encouraging others to read it. What's more, I will not cease from denouncing the clauses in the Customs Act which sanction this literary persecution in Canada as philistine and tyrannical. We are not a democracy in this country as long as such laws exist.

As I Remember

1949 March - April

At this time the projected Canadian Writers' Guild (*née* Committee) seemed coming into being. Pierre Berton, now the lively Article Editor of *Maclean's*, wrote me for a copy of the secret list of books barred from Canada, for use in a Blair Fraser article. He added that he heartily agreed with my letter in *Here & Now* about the CAA. I sent him the list and expressed the hope that "you and other writers of consequence will take some public stand for the creation of a genuine writers' guild in this country. It seems to me it can be organized only from the East and if anyone is willing to start it I am willing to do what I can out here." Berton and Lister Sinclair, in addition to Sybil Hutchinson and Joyce Marshall, were already talking up such an organization with other writers and editors, including the staff of *Here & Now*.

Launched by an honours student of English in her final year at the University of Toronto, Catherine Harmon, and a visual artist and typographer, Paul Arthur, *Here & Now's* first number had sold out almost at once on the Toronto news-stands and been hailed by Robert Weaver, along with the new *CPM*, as the joint hope for quality writing in Canadian journals. Its circulation manager, Alan Brown (one of the *Forum* poets when I was its literary editor) had arranged with me for an exchange of *Here & Now* with *CPM*, and I was also encouraging my Workshop students to take out subscriptions and submit material to it.

On the basis of letters or oral assurances I was able, by mid-April, to make a list of nearly fifty prospective Guild members with national status. There was little agreement, however, among the *ad hoc* steering committee at the *Here & Now* office as to where the guild centre should be, or who would lead it, or even whether it was to be a guild, a circle, a union, a league or a society.

Catherine Harmon wanted it focussed in Vancouver, "far enough away from the HQ of the CAA to prevent skulduggery" (O'Brien's fifth column), and me as president. *Here & Now* proposed to remain independent but supportive, supplying free legal advice, space for a Toronto branch office, and circulation of the constitution when one was forthcoming. But I was one who thought Toronto the only possible centre, and preferred Lister Sinclair for national Chairman. I was also against a mass League and for a league or academy or union of craftspeople — which was pretty well what Pelham Edgar and B.K. Sandwell had envisaged when they began the CAA!

Later in April a meeting was called in Toronto with James Scott, the

Toronto *Star* columnist, in the chair. Sybil Hutchinson reported to me that Scott credited my ghost as "officially presiding". Judging from the vague nature of the Brief which resulted, I must have been an ineffectual presence; basic organizational questions were still undecided. Don Harron, I was told, wanted headquarters in Ottawa, with P.K. Page as president, a membership concept which included "the media", and a "pressure group" policy. Berton, it seemed wanted a high-fee professional writers' and editors' union; some Montrealers wanted a low-fee high-standard academy.

While our long-conceived Guild laboured to be born, the moribund CAA went on enjoying and abusing its position as the official representative of Canadian writers. This was brought home to me once more when I consented to serve on the Governor General's Awards Committee. I was startled when the invitation came, signed by Mrs. Whyte for Deacon — the CAA and Awards board still had identical chairmen and secretaries. It seemed that Deacon must have changed his mind and decided professors might be able to guess what books the public would want to buy — in the field of poetry at least — or else he had decided I wasn't a typical professor. I began to smell a rat, however, when I learned that though Canadian publishers were free to submit for the awards whatever books they had published in the last year, the only books reaching the judges had been winnowed out by William Arthur Deacon personally and forwarded by Mrs. Whyte.

The books of poetry I received from her were all by CAA members. And there was no entry with a McClelland and Stewart imprint. Since several fine books of poetry, including Roy Daniells' first (*Deeper into the Forest*), were eligible for consideration, I wrote at once both to Mrs. Whyte, and to Sybil Hutchinson, the M&S editor, to ask why they had not been entered. Sybil replied by return mail that she had long ago submitted several M&S entries, including books by Daniells and Finch, and that she had phoned Mrs. Whyte, who had admitted they already had the books. Sybil added that she had received a similar complaint from E.K. Brown, one of the other judges in the poetry section. It was a month before Mrs. Whyte wrote me, and then only to blame M&S for failing "until now" to submit poetry books for the award. She was forwarding them at once. Knowing that Sybil Hutchinson was a woman of great integrity and a highly competent editor with no possible reason for preventing her own firm's authors from winning medals, I realized there had been yet another childish attempt in CAA headquarters to prevent the recognition of authors who did not pay fees to their decrepit society.

In April once more I was busy as an employment agent for my Creative Writing graduands. Three of them had already lined up jobs on a West Coast newspaper. Wardroper, with Klenman, drove his jalopy to

Montreal, sold it for junk, bought passage to England. Klenman followed, working his way as wet-nurse on a cattle boat. From there Wardroper began a succession of jobs on smalltown papers that were to lead him eventually to the *Manchester Guardian* and the *Times*. Klenman headed straight for the Fleet and talked himself into a job with Reuters. (He was soon to return to Canada and commence a lively career in filmmaking and television broadcasting.)

Hearing that the University of Manitoba wanted to institute a Creative Writing class, I recommended either Eric Nicol or any of my Iowa boys. Manitoba chose the young James Reaney instead, and Nicol returned from the Sorbonne to begin his long successful career as a Vancouver columnist, playwright, and national humourist.

I had been making my course accessible to editors and writers visiting Vancouver, and was happy this spring to see this policy begin to show financial as well as educational dividends. John Gray, that merry, ever-youthful man and sensitive editor, spent some days in town and charmed both my student authors and me by agreeing to set up an annual money prize for the best fiction and poetry produced annually in the Workshop. Later he was to hire one of these prize-winners, Mary MacAlpine, to begin her editorial career in his Toronto office. The Macmillan prizes were duly announced in the Calendar and people in the Bursar's office began nodding to me on the campus.

Vancouver's peach blossoms seemed to bring back its wandering writers as well as the bees. That spring of '49 saw the return of Malcolm and Margerie Lowry to their squatter's shack on the Dollarton shore, once more declaring themselves Canadians forever. We went partying there, and excited AA members met the *Volcano's* Consul. Festivities too in our Acadia shack, and at the Crawleys in Caulfeild, where I first met the wise and beautiful P.K. Page. Lister Sinclair came back "on holiday", talking with unceasing brilliance,visiting his parents and writing a dozen radio plays in between beach picnics. Pat Keatley, long since established in London as an international correspondent, and his brother Phil, about to begin a producer's life with the CBC, lazed in the May sun with us. Robert and Rita Allen arrived, she to write and he to produce plays for the Corporation, including a dramatized chapter from the novel Jim Jackson had written for me in "401". Sybil Hutchinson, in Toronto, listened to the production and asked to see the whole novel. (It was eventually published in New York under the title *To the Edge of Morning*.) Though living on Point Grey's tip, I was beginning to feel no longer marooned from my country's writers.

That spring I gave a series of talks about, and readings of, Canadian poetry to afternoon audiences in the UBC library, and through the university's Fine Arts Committee I organized a public reading by Daniells,

Livesay and myself which drew several hundred students. We were beginning to build a place on the UBC campus for the spoken poem and the resident poet.

I was also seizing whatever opportunities arose to read and comment on Canadian poetry over the air, and review magazines that published it. A dozen of these readings were recorded and transmitted to British audiences over the CBC's International Service.

On the Pacific and Mountain network I also broadcast a talk on "Canadian Magazines Today". In it I lamented the absence of a Canadian magazine of humour and of a pictorial one (thirty years later they are both still lacking) or of an equivalent for *Time* (what *Maclean's* tried to become in the seventies). In the Forties *Maclean's* had declined as a story magazine, though by '49 it was on the rise again with its new fiction editor, W.O. Mitchell. It had a rival, a modest prairie flower, the *National Home Monthly*, founded in Winnipeg by the enterprising J.K. Thomas; it bore a better quality of native story, but wilted and died within a year from prairie drought. I reminded listeners that some of the best writing, whether poetic, critical, or political, was still to be found in the *Canadian Forum*, now 28-years old and still poverty-ridden; and I lamented both the passing of Lister Sinclair's *Reading* and the survival of *Canadian Author and Bookman*, surely the dullest magazine in Canada; and I indulged personal hobbies by plugging such good and neglected magazines as the *Canadian Geographic Journal*, the *Canadian Alpine Journal*, *The Beaver*, and *Canadian Art*. What I thought were the best three literary journals I now reviewed on national radio.

Three Little Mags:
Northern Review, Contemporary Verse, Here & Now
CBC radio, 17 April 1949.

Let's have it clear at the start of this nine-minute radio race that the only things *little* about a Canadian "little mag" are its circulation and its bank balance. Of the three which I've been asked to discuss only one, *Contemporary Verse,* is even physically small and it has found space, in a couple of dozen issues, to give us nearly 400 poems. *Northern Review,* in its last four issues, devoted about 135 solid pages to the publication of prose and verse. *Here & Now,* in the three issues since its foundation a little over a year ago, has put out twice as much. It's true that, compared with what we must call a Big Magazine like *New Liberty,* the body of *Here & Now* lacks the pounds of advertising fat that make for survival. But the bones are as big, and the brain-pan really has something in it.

For these three little mags are the *primary* outlets for serious enduring literature in this country. A wider sweep than my nine minutes allow would reveal the literary role played, somewhat fitfully, by the university quarterlies and undergraduate periodicals, by *Saturday Night* and the *Canadian Forum,* and even occasionally by our popular slicks; and it would pause to salute the birth this month of a new national magazine, *Canadian Life,* which looks like a little mag of some merit trying to be a big one. But I have time only for the Biggest Little Three.

Contemporary Verse, edited by Alan Crawley from Caulfeild, B.C. and published in Victoria, with the editorial assistance of his wife and of Mrs. Floris McLaren, has presented about 80 poets, nearly all Canadian. Some have gone on to win important literary awards: Page, Gustafson, Finch, Livesay, Smith, Klein, MacKay, Marriott, F.R. Scott, and so on. Many of the others already emerging into prominence got their first chance at print through Alan Crawley's mag. That's *Contemporary Verse,* a 14-page multi-graphed quarterly, edited by a retired and sightless lawyer from his small home in the woods above West Vancouver. A journal plagued with proof errors and constant bills, asking an annual subscription price less than most of us spend for cigarettes in a week, carrying about one-tenth the advertising that you'll find in the souvenir program for a second-string college basketball game, and subscribed to by less than point one per cent of Canadians. A long-haired, white-faced little mag put out, in the words of the first editorial, "in hope to play a worthy part in the building of Canadian literature." And that is exactly what it is doing.

Northern Review, subtitled "New Writing in Canada", published and edited by John Sutherland from Montreal, is a thornier rose to grasp. To begin with, its tags are misleading. Judging by its last four issues (October 1947 to February 1949) it should be called "Eastern Review" or "New Writing as far as Stratford, Ontario." No Canadian living west of that metropolis has wormed into it since the great ruckus two years ago when seven of the thirteen founding editors resigned (including Klein, Page and Patrick Anderson). The immediate cause was not, however, Mr. Sutherland's geographic exclusiveness but what the resigning editors called his "destructive, harsh and unjust" criticism of living Canadian writers. Though Mr. Sutherland maintained that "criticism of this kind was badly needed in Canada" I notice that, since accepting the resignation of the seven, his *Northern Review* has just about bitten its tongue off trying to keep to favourable notices. To make it easier the editor has specialized in either foreign writers or books put out by his own First Statement Press. Even here it hasn't been plain sailing assessing the latest work. Of Irving Layton, one of his continuing editors and most frequent contributors, Mr. Sutherland wrote — "About three-quarters of the poems are of small value except as restoratives from our puritanical drought"....

It is only fair to say that *Northern Review* has in these four issues been consistently warm towards Canadian radio drama, National Film Board productions, and the canvases of three Montreal artists. And it has found room for experimentally interesting and sometimes vigorous poems and stories. It has the strengths of the little mag: critical independence, vitality, and the courage to present new writers, new forms, international and contemporary viewpoints. But it has not escaped the peculiar snare of the little mag either, which is provincialism, the Canadian literary disease. In some ways this is a malady of adolescence more than of environment and so may cure itself. It is family cliquism, an atmosphere of exaggerated praise and blame, but mostly blame — the suspicion of outsiders not approved by the family, plus the attitude that everybody over thirty is a stuffed-shirt and a has-been, including Pa and Ma; even big brother is on the make, and only the kid sister is enough like me to be a genius too.

Is it possible for a genuinely literary magazine, in the string of isolated communities which still make up Canada, to escape the trap? *Here & Now* may be showing the way. Published from what the masthead copy calls rather disreputable quarters in Toronto, by Paul Arthur and Catherine Harmon, it has in the three issues since its foundation made good its subtitle claim to be "A Canadian Quarterly Magazine of Literature & Art." Serious literary artists of all ages and from all parts of the country have bobbed up in it, including two Quebec writers in the French language. *Here & Now* is also unique among English-

Canadian publications, highbrow or low, in being a typographical sensation. Mr. Arthur is an earnest and gifted student of the printing craft. His type is consequently both handsome and clear, and the art-work, if occasionally dressy and self-conscious, has a lot more reason to be proud of itself than the shiny serge and dime-store trinkets which pass for make-up in most Canadian journals. The literary standards are, inevitably, up and down. The "downs" are most noticeable in the material pried from distinguished non-Canadians in an attempt to supply international *chic* without being able to pay for it. But the short story curiously mislabeled *A Chapter from a Novel* by Roy Daniells in the current issue, the poems and prose of James Reaney and others, the page-size reproductions of David Milne's paintings and E.B. Cox's wood carvings, Lister Sinclair's review of radio program music, Garrod's article on Victorian book illustrations — these in themselves have justified *Here & Now*'s existence.

But such existence, like that of the other two of these little mags, is still hand to mouth. The printers and papermakers get paid, and the bailiff is always around the corner. Is this inevitable? No. If only one-tenth of one per cent of Canadians subscribed, these magazines would be reasonably secure. Or if the Dominion Government subsidized the lot of them to the extent of one jet-propelled bomber every two years. Or one rich man gave each of them the price of a new automobile yearly. Lacking any of these, little mags struggle, die, and are reborn by succeeding idealists and innocents.

Yet it is in these journals that we print our *literature*, and always have. If you don't believe me, take a look at the magazine credits in any anthology of established Canadian writing. Take Pacey's *Book of the Canadian Short Story*, the best-known anthology of Canadian fiction at the moment. Not one of its 200-odd pieces originally appeared in the Big Mags. From Haliburton & Howe in the *Weekly Nova Scotian*, 125 years ago, and Susanna Moodie in the *Montreal Literary Garland*, to Roberts and Grove in *Queen's Quarterly*, and Irving Layton in *Northern Review* — it was the small-circulation periodicals that have given our best writers a place to hang their hats. And when no such little mags were alive Canada's authors either sent their best stuff to the United States or picked up and went there themselves. If you don't want to see that happen you can at least do one thing about it. You can subscribe to the ones trying to stay alive today.

As I Remember

1949: May-June

Once the exams were read, these months went largely in finishing the final draft of *Turvey* for McClelland & Stewart's July first deadline, and preparing a series of nine poetry readings, "The Poets Look at Canada", which Ross McLean produced from Vancouver's CBC in mid-summer. There was an AA meet to attend, where we welcomed two able author-guests, Gwladys Downes, the Victoria poet, and Jean Howarth, a Vancouver newspaper woman and fiction writer. And there were letters to ponder and answer. The news from Sybil Hutchinson was that the almost-Guild had formed a Montreal unit, and Vincent Tovell was organizing another in Toronto.

A surprise letter came, by way of the CBC, from George Woodcock, introducing himself as "a friend of Howard Sergeant (the London *Outpost* editor) and a Canadian-born English poet and biographer of . . . Godwin and Aphra Behn." He had, he said, written a review of my recent *Strait of Anian* for another London magazine but the editor had canned it. (What Woodcock didn't know was that six years before, in a Hampstead attic during a bombing raid, I had read a copy of his first book of poems, given me by a glamorous admirer of his.) George wanted to meet me and learn all about the French/English literary scene in Canada but he and his wife Ingeborg were living in a trailer in the bush on the Pacific's rim beyond Victoria, with no car to move it nearer to me.

I wrote putting him in touch with Floris McLaren, a *Contemporary Verse* editor living twenty miles from him. He replied, happy to have made this contact, and urging us to visit their trailer in July.

This was also the spring when my discontent at merely reading and writing verses and finding few ways to voice them or hear them reached the point of my writing an article urging all poets to hire halls.

Poetry Is An Oral Art: Poets Should Hire A Hall

Article; Toronto *Globe and Mail*, 22 June 1949.

Why don't Canadians read their own poets? Is it because the poets are so bad or their fellow-citizens are poetically illiterate?

What with the recent increase in the amount of verse published in Canada, and some anthologizing of our poets abroad, the notion has got around that there is a renascence of poetry in this country. The truth is that it is harder than ever to get serious verse published in Canadian periodicals, that normal book sales are not enough for the publisher to break even, that a contemporary Canadian poem is a rarity on our radio, and the barn-storming days when Carman and Roberts read their stuff in halls across the country are gone and forgotten.

Some of our best painters and novelists are starting to make a living, of sorts, selling their work. The musicians have a union (and how!), the composers get heard on the air, and every settlement of 50,000 or so has a kind of art gallery but only one bookstore in a hundred which stocks the poetry of living Canadians.

We have only two journals of verse of any standing; one is a mimeographed quarterly limited to about 1,000 lines a year; the other appears fitfully in Toronto and is consequently hostile to any verse which looks to be heterodox in either form or content. The only other journal which accepts a fair slab of poetry appears in Montreal, and is consequently hostile to any verse which looks as if it were inspired by Toronto. The other organs of culture in this country allot anywhere from 4 per cent to nothing of their space to poetry, while the amount of rhythmic utterance hidden in the draperies of a Canadian daily newspaper (and rhythmic is the best that can be said for it) never exceeds one-tenth of one per cent of the total space, much less than what is allotted for cookery, comic strips, astrology o˙ funeral notices. The big national slicks flash an occasional dime-store gem from the followers of Edgar A. Guest, but they have scarcely ever printed an example of the best in Canadian poetry.

Book sales? Excluding Service, who quite rightly does not claim to be a Canadian, the only living poet among us who sells half as well as a dozen second-rate Canadian novelists is Ned Pratt. To reach that low financial eminence Ned had to weather 20 years of buyers' neglect and become recognized abroad as perhaps the greatest narrative poet now writing in the English language. For the rest, I know two winners of Governor-General's medals (present company excepted) who have yet to sell the 500th copy of their genuinely distinguished contributions to Canadian literature.

Why? Do Canadians take it for granted that none of their ilk could possibly have written poetry worth reading unless he has died or emigrated? Personally, I don't think so. I think there is a public waiting to listen, but it will take the cooperation of a lot of different people in this country to get the poet's voice over to it.

First, the publisher. I could name ten books in as many years that were highly praised and could have sold in thousands if the publisher had risked some money on advertising.

Next, the bookseller. Poetry won't get distributed in this country until he hauls the best specimens of it from the floor-bottom shelf of his Canadian section in the back of the store and puts it in the front window with the books by non-Canadians.

Then, the literary editors. Most of them give less review-space to poets than to anybody else, and some, including the literary editor of Canada's bulkiest daily, specifically exclude Canadian poetry from their review columns. Why not give the poet some leeway, and when you print him, pay him. A 50-line poem may have taken as much time and artistry to produce as a 3,000-word short story. It is lucky if it's paid one-tenth as much; in fact, in Canada it's lucky if it's paid anything.

Next, our generous rich. We haven't many, but there are some who have endowed scholarships at universities, prizes for composers, collections of paintings for the nation. There are no national *monetary* awards for Canadian poets. I agree with Senator Athenase David of Quebec that "when Canadians learn that money-making is not the most important thing in life their native writers will have an audience."

Also, there are too many chairmen of English departments in Canadian universities who *prevent* the teaching of *modern* Canadian literature, French or English, to undergraduates. And there are too many choosers of textbooks in boards of education who are asleep to the genuine contributions Canadian poets are making. They tolerate the employment of texts and teachers whose literary influence stopped with Browning and Tennyson.

Finally, there are the poets themselves. I don't mean the jingle-ladies and jingle-lads who write rhymed lines for pin-money or parish fame, but the serious artists in words. The energy the latter use in organizing coteries and house-organs to damn each other would be better employed in creating one really good eclectic national poetry magazine or in securing a decent contract with Canadian publishers and a minimum of five cents a word for periodical publication of poetry.

Nobody will respect poets until they respect themselves. They must stop thinking they are licked from the start, that nobody wants to read them so they might as well write in such a way as is intelligible only to themselves. Sure, the public taste is bad, but it's not as low as you think. Anybody who has read modern Canadian verse publicly in this country, over the air or in a hall, knows that for every Canadian who reads a book of poetry there are a hundred more who would read if they had been properly "sold".

In any case the main thing is not to sell people books but to ensure that they *listen* to you. The great tradition of verbal poetry is a tradition of verbal music, of words arranged to be heard as well as seen. Canadian poets have got to restore that tradition, shoulder their way into radio programs and lecture recitals and make themselves known not as professors or newspapermen with a hobby for verse, but as poets and entertainers, as men and women who speak and move hearts and sway minds in an ancient and profound and mysterious way not to be achieved by any other form of art.

The trouble with Canadian poetry then, as I see it, is this gulf between the poet and his audience. The middle-men (critics, editors, publishers, patrons, etc.) can do much to narrow it, and the schools even more, but in the final analysis the challenge is to the poet himself. A lot of poets, including some of the most promising younger ones that I have met in this country, are too contemptuous of their audience. Let them stop and think that there are hundreds of thousands of people in Canada who have been educated in this generation to enjoy good music, good acting, good fiction and to a certain extent good painting. Don't tell me they can't also learn to enjoy good poetry. But before they do, a few people have to risk a little money on the poets, a lot of educators and critics have to catch up with modern modes of art, and the poets have to pluck up courage and hire a hall.

147

As I Remember

1949: July - December:

That first of July — we still called it Dominion Day — was holiday indeed for the three Birneys, the day I shipped *Turvey* to Toronto and ourselves on a ferry to Vancouver Island. In its southwest corner, where the last dirt road peters out into loggers' trails, we found the Woodcocks, beyond Sooke, "beyond France's farm, past the little saw-mill", in their bushed trailer, living off wild berries and France's turnips and advances on radio scripts and treks to the beach for clams. They were certainly impoverished, George being "between", but full of bushed exuberance, spilling over with writers' talk. I was able to suggest further CBC contacts for him and got their promise to visit us in Acadia Camp when we were back there in September.

Then we took another ferrry to Thetis Island for a blissful month of reading or writing only what I wanted to read or write, which was mainly nothing at all, four weeks of swimming and trolling and gill-netting and oyster-hunting and rowing and yakking with the islanders and sleeping in the sun.

The contact with the Woodcocks led to a long friendship. I was astonished, even awed, by his hardihood in coming to Canada with no savings or degrees or job and no intention of having one other than writing. It was obvious that he was a natural scholar and an experienced editor. His conversation flowed from a remarkable background of reading and a close acquaintanceship with leading writers in England, such as Orwell, Forster, Eliot, Herbert Read and Dylan Thomas. As soon as I began reading his books, I realized that he was a more knowledgeable and balanced literary critic than any writing in Canada. I was anxious to help him find a way to stay here.

Partly with Woodcock in mind, when I returned to Vancouver in September I bought a pile-house three down from Lowry's at Dollarton, for fifty dollars, and wrote the Woodcocks they could live in it rent-free and tax-free as long as they wanted, and let us visit them occasionally. They could then be in the Vancouver area with more chances for freelance work and more literary companionship. At the same time I began sounding out the English Department, which was looking far and wide for new staff, to discover if Woodcock could get a part-time teaching position. Just at this time, however, the department suffered a great blow in the unexpected death of its celebrated and beloved Head, Garnett Sedgewick.

Had Sedgewick lived, I am sure Woodcock would have been taken on staff at once. Although his educational standards were high he was a quick and shrewd judge of men and their abilities, never narrow-minded, neither pedant nor academic snob. Roy Daniells, who now succeeded him, was a man of considerable charm and intelligence and goodwill, but reared in a strongly Puritan faith and, at the beginning of his Headship, anxious to follow orthodox university procedures. He had little experience to help him understand a self-made biographer and philosophical anarchist like Woodcock and, in any case, he wouldn't hire anybody who did not have a B.A.

Sedgewick's death was a personal bereavement to me. For the twenty years since my father had died, Sedgewick had been a second parent. As my Head he was sometimes the benevolent despot but in essence he was the most broad-minded and considerate of chiefs. His quick mockeries were directed against the pretentious and the pedantic, and he was intolerant only of intolerance. Before I had entered his department I had been his student and his friend. I felt him to have been a truly great man, and I believed that many others shared my belief. I joined some of my colleagues in considering ways and means to set up a permanent Sedgewick lectureship at UBC , and wrote Pierre Berton, another UBC graduate and Articles Editor of *Maclean's*, asking if he would consider publishing a memorial article on Sedgewick which I would write, basing it on my memories and his letters to me. I would divert whatever payment Berton could make into the Sedgewick Memorial fund.

I was taken somewhat aback by Berton's reply, which was to the effect that Sedgewick, dead, was no longer topical, and that the public tends to lose interest in a man once he passes on. True for most men, of course, but thousands in my generation, I know, continue to revere Sedgewick's memory to this day. I felt that Pierre had become too quickly an easterner, that if Sedgewick had been Head of English at University College, Toronto, the same sense for what interests "the public" would have made Berton welcome such an article. Pierre has mellowed greatly since those days and is now one of the most humane and generous and far-seeing members of the Writers' Union of Canada — the organization which finally matured out of the Guild-egg we were all trying to lay at the end of the Forties. At that time, however, he was sharply critical of writers whose work had achieved no popular or commercial success, and his attitude, I believe, coming head-on against the idealism of writers like Joyce Marshall, was one of the reasons why the great many writers who were united in rejecting the CAA could not in 1949 find a common positive ground for a new union.

I was still clinging to the hope that the talented young editors of *Here & Now* could work with *Maclean's* editors like Berton to cement our disparate members. The effects of my letter of resignation from the CAA in the second number of *Here & Now* had certainly been widespread. It had even, Harmon wrote me, goaded a CAA member into stealing his way up a coal chute into the *Here & Now* office after it was closed for the day, and challenging its editor to a "duel". I felt certain that nothing so dramatic was likely to happen in Bourinot's CPM office. The latest indication I had received of the editorial boldness of that magazine was a letter from Norman Levine quoting a rejection slip he had received from Bourinot, returning a mild satire Levine had sent him on "Canadian culture". "I like it," Bourinot had scribbled, "but I can't publish it, not in a national magazine." So Levine had sent it to Chicago *Poetry* , which promptly printed it.

But there were ominous signs that *Here & Now* was mounting money-trouble. Although the second number jumped their circulation from a thousand to fifteen hundred, Harmon wrote me their deficit for the year "will be about $3,000" and that she was appealing to Frank Scott and other Montreal poets to find her support from the Southam Fund. I replied I was finding it difficult to get subs for *Here & Now* in Vancouver because of increasing rumours that Arthur was resigning to go to England. Arthur himself then wrote me that *Here & Now* was on sound financial ground, the printer paid, the deficit down to $300. On this basis I continued getting subs, reviewed the magazine over two CBC radio programs, and gave it poems and the first chapter of *Turvey* without fee. By 1950, however, *Here & Now* was gone forever.

The opening of fall term in September involved me once again in the exciting but difficult task of reducing a hundred or more applications for "401" to a score of accepted students for the 49-50 academic year. Among those I chose was a long fellow with a devil-may-care look about him who had submitted, as a proof of his ability to write creatively, a parody of my "David". He had been "forced", he said, looking at me slantwise, "to study the poem in Matric." It was a remarkable burlesque, almost thirty stanzas duplicating, without faltering, both the assonance and the half-rhyming of my five-beat line. He had told much the same story but with the essential difference that his hero, Saul, preferred life in a wheelchair to death on the ice, and had to be relentlessly shoved over the rest of the cliff by a meticulously romantic Bob. I welcomed such a shrewd satirist to the class. But he wrote nothing after half so good. His name was Tom Franck; the last I saw of him was a few years ago on an American TV "experts" panel, where he was introduced as a distinguished professor of international law. He looked as lanky as ever, and even more quizzical.

There were two others in this class equally talented and a joy to have: George Robertson, already an AA member, and Daryl Duke. Botl. have since made important contributions to "the media". Daryl Duke, who wrote poems for the student magazine, became for a while a producer of talk-shows in Hollywood, but returned to Canada and is now, with Klenman, part owner of a Vancouver television station.

That autumn I succeeded, after many attempts, in getting an American poet of some status to visit our Workshop. The difficulty had been the total lack of funds available from either the students or the administration to pay a poet. I had been corresponding occasionally for about seven years with Kenneth Rexroth, an advisory editor for the New Directions Press. He had first written me about my poem "David". Later I read and admired his second book of verse, *The Phoenix and the Tortoise*, and now in '49 he had brought out a third collection of his work and an anthology, *The New British Poets*, also from the prestigious New Directions Press of James Laughlin in Connecticut. Rexroth, however, was quite unknown to UBC's English department, even to the professor who gave the only courses in "contemporary literature". I got Rexroth to come, nevertheless, by paying myself for his return bus ticket from San Francisco, and guaranteeing him bed and board with me while he was in Vancouver — in return for his giving one unpaid reading of his poetry in the university library. The English Department would not sponsor or even publicize the event, but Authors Anonymous, as a valid campus club (with no treasury), was allowed to do it.

Two or three of the forty-odd English teachers turned up and clapped politely at the end, but every student writer on the campus was there, and their positive responses made it all worthwhile, for Rexroth and for me. I felt that AA and "401" had got up enough speed at last to get to the other side of the Waste Land syndrome, and I was pleased to find that our Contemporary Literature man had started travelling with us. With his help we now began planning ways to finance bringing up Dylan Thomas to our auditorium when and if his projected American tour came off in 1950.

Meantime, I was happy to discover that Harry Boyle, visiting Vancouver from CBC's national office, was willing to come up to the campus and spend a couple of hours with my Workshop. Unaffected, plain-spoken, jovial and immensely knowledgeable about radio writing, Harry's short visit increased considerably my students' opinion of the value of professional media careers in Canada.

By the year's end I was getting invitations myself to read, for *Turvey* was out and being, on the whole, favourably reviewed. I was imported to a Victoria bookstore to sign copies at a bee, and there I met, among others, a lissome and enigmatic young lady who was beginning to write most original and sensitive lyrics. Her name was Phyllis Webb and she was later to join the English department at UBC first as a student and then as a teacher. I have continued to admire her and her poetry ever since.

In December I was asked by the CBC to review Knister's posthumous *Collected Poems* and James Reaney's first book. I have written earlier of meeting Knister. Reaney I became aware of in 1946 when I came

151

across some of his verses in the University of Toronto's *Undergrad*. Shortly after, I met him at a Toronto party given me by Sybil Hutchinson; he was still a Varsity sophomore, but a very unusual one. I've never forgotten the impression he made on me that evening — a small packet of firecrackers set alight, he went sizzling and leaping mischievously from one guest to another, an excited child popping adult questions, bouncing into the kitchen and back to the hall, and continually exploding with ideas, images and emotions. I thought him a marvelously inventive Ariel, and still do. The next year Sybil sent me the early chapters of a novel he was writing. I thought it showed him capable of writing successful adult satire as well as grown-up juveniles, but I wondered if he would learn to shed his dilettantish neglect of form, a willingness to let a sloppy sentence stay if it carried a novel image. His adolescent brilliance was almost a danger to him, dazzling most critics and lulling him into fixating his immaturities. His later work proved me over-critical, and I had failed to perceive the very adroit playwright lurking in him.

I continued, though, to prefer his poems. I had published some of them in CPM and had been much amused to receive a lengthy complaint about them from a laboratory assistant in his university. The lady had gone to the trouble of mimeographing and circulating the poems to "fifty highly-trained and rather brilliant government biologists". Like her, "they did not believe that that was poetry". Nor did her father, an electrical engineer, nor her "old high-school teacher in English", nor "every student at the U. of T." she had "discussed the matter with". Did I think "James Reaney wrote logical or reasonable poetry? I grant him . . . a terrifying and sometimes beautiful imagination and there is no doubt that he is a rare being, a genius — but never would I consider that he is a poet." His genius, she went on, was for "pointed criticism". It seems that she had shown him some of her poems and he had pointed holes in them. And then one he had liked she had sent to CPM and I had accepted it and it hadn't come out!

I was able to tell her that it was predictable O'Brien, back in the Toronto offices of CPM, who had cut her poem out of the dummy at the last minute, for reasons not disclosed to me, and that if he relented it might appear in the next number. But I also congratulated her on her excellent description of Reaney's talents and shortcomings. They were exactly what made him, for me, a good poet, but an unlikely government biologist.

About Reaney and Knister

Review of *The Red Heart* by James Reaney and the *Collected Poems* of Raymond Knister; 14 December 1949.

The two new books of Canadian poetry which I've been asked to talk about today both happen to be the work of lonely young men writing from the physical viewpoint of small Ontario farms. But there the resemblance stops and the differences are so sharp as to be symbolic of what has been happening to Canadian poetry and Canadian ways of life within a generation.

For the poems of Raymond Knister*, now for the first time collected, were written twenty-five to thirty years ago. Knister was a shy, bookish only-son of respectable Methodist farmers; at seven he developed a stammer which afflicted him till his death at thirty-two.

But he could write, and before he was well out of his teens, he had produced some distinguished poems and tales. No one in Canada, however, would publish them. They were, as he rightly said later, "so Canadian, and came so directly from the soil, that Canadian editors would have nothing to do with them." In other words, they weren't about just autumn maples and shy fauns and noble vanished redmen; they were about oat crops and swilling pigs and sweating farmers. They were, if you like, the things Sarah Binks was to write about too, but they were, and are, genuine poems, not parodies, written with a sombre honesty and in a style as simple, direct and pliant as the leather reins with which he drove his Clydesdales. In "Stable-Talk" we hear the horses themselves:

"We have sweat our share; the harrow is caught full of sod-pieces, the bright disks are misted yellow in the wet. Hear tardy hesitant drips from the eaves! . . . Let the dozy eye, the one raised hip, give no hint to the hours. . . . We are not done with toil: let rain work in these hours, wind in night's hours. We with the sun together, tomorrow. . . ."

How Knister finally found publication for poems like these in American quality magazines, moved to the U.S. and wrote for the famous *Midland* — and came back to the Ontario farm because it was Canada he wanted to write about; how he struggled to keep himself and family on the earnings of a Toronto hackwriter and yet found time to write novels, plays, criticism and short stories that were not hackwriting, is itself a story to move us all. It is told by his friend and editor, the poet Dorothy Livesay, in a memoir prefacing the book. It's a good memoir, understanding, full, and careful. Both Miss Livesay and her publishers, the Ryerson Press, are to be thanked for a work that would obviously never be a big seller but which will add another stone to the foundation of a permanent Canadian literature.

It's a small stone, granted. Knister's was a limited personality; his poetic technique is largely confined to that kind of rural understatement and casualness which Robert Frost used more richly, or to the rather monotonously-etched free verse of the Imagists. He had little of what we call high spirits, and not enough, to be an important poet, of the capacity for image-making or thoughtful fantasy. But he was an honest objective artist and a pioneer in Canadian realism and he deserved a better fate than to live a short unhappy life, and die by drowning seventeen years before Canada printed his poems.

Mr. James Reaney, the author of *The Red Heart*, was also, as I've said, an Ontario farm boy, lonely — an only child — bookish, shy, and a practising writer from adolescence. But he had the luck, from a literary point of view, of being born in the late twenties instead of in 1899. With the help of scholarships, he got what poverty and ill health stopped Knister from getting, a University of Toronto education, and he is, at present at least, freed from a hackwriter's fate, for he is already an assistant professor teaching Creative Writing in the University of Manitoba — a job which in Knister's generation had not yet been thought of. Moreover, though Reaney's verse and prose are just as unusual, and therefore as shocking, to most editors of popular Canadian magazines today as Knister's were in his day (what commercial Canadian magazine has ever really "discovered" an important Canadian author?), Reaney has not had to go outside our borders for recognition. He has published in *Here & Now* and other Canadian little magazines of this generation. And now, while Reaney is still quite young and very much alive, a Canadian publisher, McClelland and Stewart, has brought out a first collection of his poems, in the handsome Indian File series. Anyone who fails to read this book will miss the most refreshing reading offered by a Canadian poet in many moons.

For Mr. Reaney, though he may lack some of Knister's mature selectivity and restraint, has just about everything that Knister was short on: verbal gusto and wit, concentrated imaginativeness, an original and satanic sense of humour, virtuosity in metrical sleight-of-hand, an ear for satire, and that profoundly childlike eye and mind which sees in a ripe plum on a tree both a blue pendulum thrumming the gold-wire winds of summer and an emblem of approaching death, the mortality even of the stars. The trees and animals of the farm, the old school globe dusty in the attic, the village poetess, the roaring highway beyond, are simply points of departure, explosive centres, for thoughts that reach out to the farthest sun and into its red heart and his own:

"My red heart hangs heavily and will never fall loose, but grow so heavy after only a certain number of seasons... that it will bring bough, tree, and the fences of my bones down to a grave in the forest of my still upright fellows... So does the sun hang now from a branch of Time in this wild fall sunset. Who shall pick the sun from the tree of Eternity?... It seems that no one can, and so the sun shall drag gods, goddesses and parliament buildings, Time, Fate, gramaphones and Man to a gray grave where all shall be trampled beneath the dancing feet of crowds of other still-living suns and stars."

There is so much that is exciting in this book, and technically new in Canadian poetry. For me, the most original and memorable pieces are the comic fantasies, lighter than the Websterian death pieces, but no more trivial really than a Klee painting or a vignette by Kafka. "Klaxon" is one of these:

"All day cars mooed and shrieked, hollered and bellowed and wept upon the road. They slid by with bits of fur attached, fox-tails and rabbit-legs, the skull and horns of deer; cars with yellow spectacles, or motorcycle monocle; cars whose gold eyes burnt with a too-rich battery... chariots from whose foreheads leapt silver women of ardent bosom. Ownerless, passengerless, driverless, they came to anyone and with headlights full of tears begged for a master, for someone to drive them... Automobiles begged of posts the whereabouts of their mother. But no one wished to own them any more. Everyone wished to walk."

1949: Coda 31 December

(On the last day before the Fifties I wrote down, for a Toronto literary friend, a somewhat haphazard assessment of myself, and kept a carbon. Some extracts from it seem to me, thirty years later, to provide an ending to this first half of *Spreading Time*.)

Who was I? The only child of British-born immigrants. My first seven years on a remote ranch in the Alberta bush. That shaped me to be at home with "Nature" — animals, flowers in the summer sun, the vast snows of winter — and to be shy of humans. A Wordsworthian infant but precociously literate. Everything happened within a radius of ten miles. The villages of Ponoka, Lacombe, glimpsed once or twice on the rim. Morningside flag station a half-hour weekly buggy ride from the ranch-house, the centre. A world without cars, phones, planes, tractors, electricity, plumbing...

Around us a scattering of peoples through the bush, immigrants from Europe, some without English, some Métis, Indians wandering from the reserve, Americans from the Dakotas. But as far back as I can remember all this was a part of something important called Canada, itself a circle inside a huge one called the British Empire, which was almost the whole world, and had a King called Edward the Seventh who was on all our stamps. Except for China and Africa, where someday I could go as a missionary doctor, my mother said. She and my father had a little schooling and always worked hard, but now, in Canada we had a farm and soon we would not be so poor because things always got better in Canada.

And Canada was something more than farms. My mother sang me Scottish songs, but my father read me Lampman. They took me in the sleigh with them when they went to a barn-dance. I learned to read from the Montreal *Family Herald* and the Toronto Sundayschool paper and Eaton's catalogue. But when the farm didn't give enough food, my father moved us to Banff and began housepainting again.

A second seven-years, now in the mountain tourist village. I needed above all to be accepted by the animal pack of the schoolyard, but I was a dub at hockey, went alone speedskating on the river, roamed the mountainsides in summer. I couldn't run with the gang because I couldn't help wanting to learn in my head, and so I got shameful high marks. Above all I loved reading and writing, I read whatever came my way, read Canadian books with no thought about who wrote them, except that sometimes they were about places and happenings my parents knew. I grew to realize my Canada was huge and full of strangeness, big enough to include the Calgary *Herald* and the Calgary *Eye-Opener*, the Limberlost and Glengarry, the Riel rebellion, Labrador and Service's Yukon. And a World War my father went to, while I learned to sell news of it. And sell anything else a tourist would buy from me... I became a fourteen-year-old not-so-innocent Grade Niner waiting to be a tough mountain guide and packer. Then my father moved us to a berry-farm on a remote hillside in the Kootenays. Finishing my Matric in a one-room highschool, I became stronger, the catcher for the baseball team, not so frightened now of girls. But I kept on leading my class, began writing verses in secret... This farm's soil was even poorer than Morningside's. After two years my father sold again and moved back to Banff.

Two years then on my own, an itinerant labourer, no longer dreaming much of being anything else, in solitude scribbling bad verses and burning them, beginning to imagine scenes for plays, novels — but wisely telling myself no one could make a living doing that in Canada. My mother's ambition, to go to a university, nevertheless is transferred to me. At eighteen I'd saved enough, and came to UBC.

Another eight years being educated, learning not to *write* but to *teach* writing — for that was the rewarded skill. The first thing to remember was that Canadian writing was not worth teaching. Second, there were lifetime careers in Canada or the States for someone who had degrees and could teach Caedmon's Hymn and *Piers Plowman*, or the *Faerie Queene*, or Dryden's heroic tragedies. Oddly, some of those eight years had to be spent in an American university. There, in sight of the meal-ticket, I was rolled with everyone else into the swamp of the Depression, and felt lucky to have a temporary job teaching bonehead composition in a backward midwest college.

So I taught, taught well, to no avail, either to the students or myself. I was assured I would soon be dropped, and was.... Came back to Canada, where there were only the Relief Camps. And became a Marxist... for another seven years. A schizoid professor sneaking Marx and Kautsky into the *Canterbury Tales* in class and, off campus, a seditious citizen of the world revolution, self-sworn to write only what can help the Cause. A Trotskyist literary editor for the social-reformist *Canadian Forum*. I convert myself to the cause of Canadian creativity.

Marriage, fatherhood, another World War turn me out of that dichotomy to another. I am declared a poet (albeit only a Canadian one) and an infantry officer (albeit only a psychologist)...

The war won, perhaps, but the Canadian revolution indefinitely postponed, I return to Canada as restless a man as my long-dead father. The job waiting in Toronto is a small plush coffin I refuse. I try a brass hat for size, in the Media. It slides over my ears, smothers. I go back to professoring, back to my alma mater, the West Coast, but on condition I can have one "course" I can believe in, the first stone in a little shelter for the creative student naked in academia.

That stipulation was the wisest I, a foolish man in general, ever made. The feeling of companioning and actually helping talented young writers to survive and mature still sustains me after three years here at UBC. Years of overcrowded classrooms, insufficient help, miserly salary, sinking academic standards. And two years of wasting my time and my spirits trying to make a sow's ear of a magazine into a silk purse for the Canadian Authors Association. A folly I had anticipated and yet failed to resist. I think it was those two silly Governor-General's medals turned my head, made me think I could be the irresistible editor . . .

Now I sit here in my middle-class living room on the last day of the Forties, wondering what I can be in the Fifties . . . But who am I now? A poet, yes, but belated, not happy with what I've written. Six weeks ago my novel came out and has already gone to a second printing, sold more copies than my three books of poetry have sold together in seven years. I want to write another, not the "sequel" my publishers want, but something big, serious, about the Depression. I want to write more criticism, start my own magazine, write plays.

But what I must go on doing is teaching. I would have to write two *Turveys* a year if I were to support my family as a fulltime writer. And though I can teach under compulsion I can't write under it. Yet teaching is getting more burdensome here for everybody. The new Head is increasing my already heavy workload, and the university is putting me on more and more committees . . . I have a standing invitation to join the English Department at the University of Washington in Seattle; I would have time there to revise my doctoral thesis, publish, become known across the scholars' world as a Chaucerian, get a Guggenheim, etc. But I don't want to stop being a Canadian. I may be forced to. The one course I give that's worth the giving is the one the Head won't let me enlarge, even threatens to plow under: Creative Writing. There is not even, here at UBC, a half-course in Canadian literature. And the one course on so-called "contemporary literature" contains nothing written after the Thirties. Like the *Poems of Today* text when I came here as a freshman.

So long as I stay here I must fight for the creative principle in education, and against the clinging colonial distrust of its own talents. I must find more good souls like John Gray to endow prizes, scholarships, extra courses for young writers to come to UBC. I've begged in vain from the women's clubs, poetry societies, alleged patrons of the arts in this Philistine loggers' town. And from the provincial government. I'll have to campaign in the east, in Ottawa maybe. . . .

Soon it will be midnight. Where do I go from here? Where do all of us who try to be critics and teachers and cultivators of artistic talent go? We all know Canada grows the best Number One Hard Wheat. Have we no soil for Number One Hard Poetry? To ask such questions betrays what a fool I am and have been since childhood. I think of myself as an internationalist still. Why should I worry then if this artificially separated hunk of land and water between the 49th parallel and the North Pole never becomes a real nation with its own cultural identity? CanLit may *never* be worth sounding off about; in the whole country today we haven't more than a half-dozen genuine artists of poetry. The rest of them, myself included, are versifying fools, caught in academic traps we helped to forge and cannot spring. Have I the guts to pry my steel jaws apart?

What rant! What pretentious and hackneyed prose I write! I'm supposed to have a sense of humour. Let me remember Sarah Binks, let me be content to ride the manure wagons, fork in hand, scattering my critical cowshit over the marginal farmland, so that Sarah may delight in the golden flecks, and sing,

> I'm a genius, I'm a genius...
> I toot upon my little flute,
> And twang upon my lyre.

Come in, 1950!

***

END OF BOOK ONE

Index (to Canadian references)